ARISTOPHANES

BIRDS

∞

A rhyming verse translation

by

Greg Fraser

Published by
QUIDZUNC

Most versions of this play are for the birds. This one's for you!

Here, for the first time, even those without the mastery of Ancient Greek will come as close as the Greeks themselves to speaking the language of the gods, and to understanding the songs of birds...

Originally published as an appetizer to a Greek-English interlineal version of the play – with which it was coupled in a single, large-format volume – this pocketbook edition has been slimmed down, but still includes the customized glossary of explanatory notes from the earlier edition, offering tidbits and insights once only ever glimpsed from the dizzying heights of Cloudcuckooland itself...

Oh, and a warning: This book contains fowl language.

Also in this series

Pocketbook translations in rhyming verse:

Aristophanes, *Peace*

Aristophanes, *Armysundua* (forthcoming)

Aristophanes, *Clouds* (forthcoming)

ΟΡΝΙΘΕΣ

∞

ΑΡΙΣΤΟΦΑΝΗΣ

αἱ Χάριτες τέμενός τι λαβεῖν ὅπερ οὐχὶ πεσεῖται διζόμεναι,
The Graces, wanting to hold a sanctuary that would never fall,
ψυχὴν εὗρον Ἀριστοφάνους.
found the soul of Aristophanes.

Cover illustration & design by Alison Mutton
ISBN 978-1-7640582-0-9

Pocketbook edition
first published by QUIDZUNC, April 2025

Title: Aristophanes Birds
ISBN 978-1-7640582-0-9 (pbk.)
Subjects: Aristophanes
Birds (play)
Ancient Greek comedy
Author/Contributors:
Fraser, Greg
Aristophanes
Mutton, Alison (illustrator)
Series: Aristophanes: Pocketbook translations in rhyming verse, no. 2 – Birds

A catalogue record for this work is available from the National Library of Australia

Synopsis:

A free rhyming verse translation of Aristophanes' *Birds.* Includes a fully customized glossary of explanatory notes.

Contents

About this book

This book is a pocket-sized version of the rhyming verse translation of Aristophanes' BIRDS – his most popular comedy – originally published as *Part One* of the large-format Greek-English interlineal volume of the same name.

While the interlineal format of its forerunner was designed to give all those wishing to read, play, sing, or study the work of Aristophanes access to some of the complexity of his many puns, allusions, and double-meanings – joys that, despite the work of generations of translators, editors, poets, and producers, are denied those without the benefit of fluency in the Attic Greek of ancient Athens – the aim of this edition is simply to give newcomers to Aristophanes a real taste of Aristophanic wit and whimsy – as opposed to the rather stilted product that invariably arises from an attempt at strict literalism – and hence perhaps the motivation to further exploration of this wonderful poet. Those wishing to know the strict literal meaning of Aristophanes' original are referred to the Greek-English interlineal version of the play, which has been slimmed-down too, and is available as a stand-alone text in the pocketbook companion to the present edition. Ultimately however, the essence of poetry, comedy, and theatre, lies in its immediacy, and no amount of commentary, gloss, or creativity can ever hope to translate the untranslatable.

To this end, this version of the play merely tries to convey something of the *emotional* impact – rather than just the dry literal sense – of Aristophanes upon his audience. This of course is a balancing act. No translator is free to simply freelance, but where the literal sense of the words in translation is no longer immediately and emotively "intelligible", I have chosen to discard literalism altogether, and have substituted in an idiom, cliché, joke, pun, or explicatory phrase designed to be faithful to the clever flow of fun, lyric, and edification so essential to what Aristophanes must have represented to his original audience. In particular, I have substituted proper names quite freely, as the preservation of an obscure reference is not Aristophanic, whereas the inclusion of an anachronism here and there certainly is.

The stage directions are all mine, and I have sometimes indulged rather lengthy interpolations to explain obscure or ambiguous points, and consequently the line numbers are an approximate guide only.

And, for newcomers to Old Comedy, a tip: What you are about to experience was originally not simply a play, nor a musical, nor even just a "comedy" as we now understand such things to be; it was all of these things, but also part of a religious festival, a theatrical competition, and a spectacular of song and dance written and performed according to a (reasonably flexible) set of customs and cultural expectations; the chorus plays a central role, the protagonists often "break the fourth wall", and ribaldry and satire clothe the plot. Expect the unexpected, because nothing can ever again be newer than the first things of their kind: the masterworks of the original master himself: Aristophanes.

I hope you enjoy your flight!

– G.F.

BIRDS

freely, after

ARISTOPHANES

∞

Dramatis Personae

Greenhorn (an Athenian)
Silvertongue (an Athenian)
Hoopoe's Manservant
Tereus (once a human King, now the Hoopoe)
The Nightingale (once Prokne, wife to Tereus)
A Chorus of Various Birds
The Leader of the Chorus (An Owl)
A Priest
A Poet
An Oraclemonger
Meton (a famous geometer)
An Inspector
A Decree Seller
First Messenger
Second Messenger
Iris (the Rainbow)
Herald
A Parricide
Kinesias (a well-known inferior poet)
An Informer
Prometheus
Poseidon
Herakles
Trumpianus (a barbarian god)
Sovereigntina
Various Slaves & Attendants

A WILDERNESS, SOMEWHERE OUTSIDE ATHENS, AROUND THE TIME
OF THE PEACE OF NICIAS (421 B.C.).
THERE IS A LARGE TREE AT THE BACK, WITH A THICKET TO EACH SIDE.
GREENHORN AND SILVERTONGUE ENTER, EACH CARRYING A BIRD
TETHERED TO HIS ARM, AND FOLLOWED BY A SLAVE CARRYING LUGGAGE.

GREENHORN
"Straight ahead!", my jay just said, to where that tree, er...
seems to be...
SILVERTONGUE
No, ow! Bugger me dead... this thing's crowing for us to head
back the way we came!
GREENHORN
What birds are we! – weaving in and out and to and fro'...
We're bringing ourselves undone, you know,
looking for this, er... "other" way to go.
SILVERTONGUE
Oh no, the prize is mine alone: I've gone 'round this track
a thousand times already, persuaded by this crow!
GREENHORN
And this jay has conned me into wearing the tips off every toe!
SILVERTONGUE
That's bad enough, but where on earth we are...
I just simply do not know!
GREENHORN
Well, can you tell if we're still in Attika? I haven't got a clue.
SILVERTONGUE
I'm no more certain, by god, than Jonah...
GREENHORN
...the Wandering Jew? – We're lost souls, then.
SILVERTONGUE
Well, this is hardly the path well-trod, my friend.
GREENHORN
Oh, what a prank that bloke from the bird-market played,

the bastard, on me and you... when he said these birds would send us straight to Tereus...

SILVERTONGUE

... he swore it black and blue!

GREENHORN

"to the Hoopoe, you'll go" he said...

SILVERTONGUE

..."to the bird that was a king..."

GREENHORN

...though now he's king of the birds!

SILVERTONGUE

And we bought it!

GREENHORN

Them. And this one can't even sing!
That one cost me half-a-buck, and this one he threw in "for luck", and they know nothing apart from pecking... Ow! what the...
now what are you gawking?

SILVERTONGUE

Is it "Head down off those rocks?"

(RUNS TO THE EDGE OF THE STAGE AND PEERS OVER)

GREENHORN

Or "Head first off those rocks!"

SILVERTONGUE

But there's no way! So I say: "No way!" That ain't the straight-an'-narrow...

GREENHORN

Well, what's that crow got to say for itself?
Listen: it's stopped its squawking!

SILVERTONGUE

You're right, by Zeus: it's changed its tune...
now it's chirping like a sparrow!

GREENHORN

A little tidbit about which way to go?

SILVERTONGUE
Well, ow! No. He says he can peck my fingers
clean down to the marrow!
GREENHORN (TO THE AUDIENCE)
Not bad really, is it, for us to be bound, and all set to go
to the crows – but now we can't even find the way!
Listen up then: a word of advice, for all youse who've lost the plot,
like us, and come here to this play –
let me tell you what's driving us on... We're homesick!
Not away from home and wishing we weren't,
but when being at home we wished we were gone
to almost anywhere that didn't make us sick of being in the city.
Yes, we're city-folk, Athenians, proud citizens, patriotic,
well-bred, but tired of the urban nitty-gritty... No, not neurotic,
not run-out-of-town, nor scared into flight from a nation
so great and by nature well-blessed... where everything's fair
and everyone there gets to pay fees in unending litigation.
No, Athens is best... why, though her cicadas sing for a month or two,
the Athenians sing their whole lives through... in lawsuits
and artful equivocation... So that's why we're trekking this trail,
with pots and myrtle for the due consecration... of a new place to live –
a place without trials and travail, and far from the madding crowd.
So we're fully equipped and now just looking for Tereus, the hoopoe,
because we're sure that he will know... having seen some such place
in one of his foraging-flights...
SILVERTONGUE
Hey!
GREENHORN
What is it?
SILVERTONGUE
The crow's looking up.
GREENHORN
And things are looking up with this jay bird too!

Maybe there are some birds up there?
SILVERTONGUE
In a tree? Well, I suppose they're not afraid of heights.
I tell you what: we'll soon see... if we make a little noise.
Get hopping, and give that rock a kick.
GREENHORN
No, use your head, man: that'll double the yelp!
SILVERTONGUE
Alright then, take a stone and knock on wood.
GREENHORN
By all means, if you think it'll help...
(TAKES A STONE AND TAPS OUT A RHYTHM ON A TREE TRUNK)
"O Te-reus! O Te-reus!"
SILVERTONGUE
Hold it! Hold it! That's no good! – What are you saying here?
"Oh Terry us, so Terry us?" Why, that won't work at all... Why,
don't you know: "Oh Boy! Oh Boy!" is more like the Hoopoe's call!
GREENHORN
"O Boy! O Boy!" Really? Well, I didn't know.
Here, let me try again. "O Boy! O Boy!"

HOOPOE'S MANSERVANT (ENTERS FROM BEHIND THE TREE)
Who is it? Who's calling my master then?
SILVERTONGUE
Good god deliver us! It's the yawning gap!
(FARTS, AND HOLDS HIS BOTTOM CLENCHED)
HOOPOE'S MANSERVANT (FLAPPING AGGRESSIVELY)
Good god deliver us! It's bird-snatchers!
GREENHORN
Good god deliver us! I think I've done a crap...
HOOPOE'S MANSERVANT
(SETTLING DOWN TO INSPECT THE VISITORS' BACKSIDES)
Hmm, you intruders seem to have come unstuck!

SILVERTONGUE
But we're not intruders.
HOOPOE'S MANSERVANT
Well, you look like men: what are you then?
SILVERTONGUE
Why, we're just like you, we're birds too,
and I am a Featherless Fearling: a bird you just can't pluck.
HOOPOE'S MANSERVANT
You're talking shit.
SILVERTONGUE
Not talking: it's running down my leg!
HOOPOE'S MANSERVANT
Hmm, I think you're pulling mine...
(TO GREENHORN) *Well, what sort of bird are you?*
Or can't you speak? You don't have a beak...
GREENHORN
Why, I am a Beakless Brown-tail.
SILVERTONGUE
But what sort of bird are you then?
You're obviously not a quail...
HOOPOE'S MANSERVANT
I'm a buttle-bird.
SILVERTONGUE (LOOKING AROUND TO THE MANSERVANT'S TAIL)
Well, that is a helluva butt. So you're not a cock, I take it?
HOOPOE'S MANSERVANT
No, and I don't. I'm the butler, the hoopoe's head manservant;
he took me along when he became a bird,
to save himself from all the huttle and the buttle...
SILVERTONGUE
But that's absurd! Does a bird even need a servant?
HOOPOE'S MANSERVANT
This one does, inasmuch, I suppose, as being once a king,
always a king, or however that saying goes –

You see, now and then he loves to eat Phalerian small fry:
so I take a bowl and fetch a few sardines.
But if he sets his heart on soup, I fetch a pot and spoon,
I fly the coop... and hey-diddle-diddle...
GREENHORN
...you jump over the moon?
SILVERTONGUE
So, you're a fetching bird. Well then, your master:
you should fetch him for us.
HOOPOE'S MANSERVANT
But he's taking a nap... having just devoured some myrtle-berries
– and quite a few gnats – I can't wake him up so soon.
GREENHORN
Well, wake him all the same.
HOOPOE'S MANSERVANT
But I know he won't be happy.
Still, since you seem to have lost your flocks, I will go...
and interrupt his napping. (EXITS TO THE THICKET)
SILVERTONGUE (CALLING AFTER HIM)
And go to hell too! – Why, he gave me a helluva fright...
GREENHORN
Oh, now bugger me: the crow's shot through...
er: he's taken flight...
SILVERTONGUE
Oh, you chicken, so you really did "let fly"?
GREENHORN
Hey, but where's your jay? Didn't you "let go" too?
SILVERTONGUE
Oh no, by Zeus, not I!
GREENHORN
Where is it then?
SILVERTONGUE
It flew away... of its own accord. Discretion, you know,

is the better fart of pallor...
GREENHORN
Oh, "He who farts and flies away..."?
SILVERTONGUE
Yes, "...he lives to fart another day!"
TEREUS (WITHIN)
Open the thicket, so I can come out already!

THE SLAVES PART THE THICKET, AND TEREUS ENTERS

GREENHORN
O Herakles! The beast has flown the nest! –
SILVERTONGUE
...and his feather's are all messed...
TEREUS
Who are they, seeking me?
SILVERTONGUE
...and what's with the outlandish triple crest?
The twelve gods seem to have done you over.
TEREUS
Surely you're not mocking me for my plumage?
Know ye, O Strangers, I was once a king.
GREENHORN
Oh no, we'd never laugh at a king's plumage.
TEREUS
At what then?
GREENHORN
Well, that beak of yours is a silly-looking thing!
TEREUS
Thus however Sophokles disgraces me, Tereus, in his tragedies.
GREENHORN
So you are Tereus? Man or bird: which?
TEREUS
I am a king...fisher... well, a hoopoe, actually.

GREENHORN
Well then, where are your feathers?
TEREUS
I lost them in the switch... from man to bird.
GREENHORN
Why, what went wrong?
TEREUS
Nothing, all birds drop feather in the change of season
and look a little shabby till some new ones come along.
But tell me: Who are you two?
GREENHORN
Who? Us? We're mere mortals.
TEREUS
Kin from what country?
GREENHORN
We're from the land whose gleaming galleys
boast triple-rows of port'oles!
TEREUS
Not jurymen, I hope?
GREENHORN
Nope! Why, we're just the opposite: We're juryphobiacs.
TEREUS
Do tell! That's a seed I've never seen in any Athenian field.
GREENHORN
Well, a search for such seed is a very low yield, er... operation.
TEREUS
So, in the matter of... you have come here wanting...?
GREENHORN
Why, we're seeking – with you – to make a brief consultation.
TEREUS
About what? Since when?
GREENHORN
Since previously you were a man, like us now;

and you owed money, like us now;
and you were not pleased to repay, like us now;
and then... transformed to a nature like unto the birds,
and flying rings around the earth and sea...
who better could we beg for an informed reconnaissance,
and a few wise words – you having taken in so much as men
and seen so far as birds? – So we pray thee...
O Tereus: can you point us out a cosy city
where we can bed-down, like in a soft coverlet,
without a daily plea?

TEREUS

Of innocence? Are you seeking a city of justice...
greater than Athens?

GREENHORN

No, not greater, but better adjusted... to just us.

TEREUS

Then you are clearly seeking an aristocracy.

GREENHORN

Oh no, not at all! Aristo-phanes doesn't mix with hypo-crisy.

TEREUS

In what sort of place, then, would you most like to dwell?

GREENHORN

Well... what about one where the most troublesome thing
might be one of my friends at the door, just as the day is aborning,
saying "by Zeus on Olympus, both you and the kids be at my hearth
bright-and-early first thing in the morning...
I'm about to host a wedding" he'll say, "so take an early bath,
and don't do another thing all day" – that is: I'll be welcome
empty-handed – and the moreso even more gladly!
And if I don't show, he lets me know... er, that I'm still welcome...
except when he's doing badly!

TEREUS

By Zeus, you do like it rough! And what about you?

SILVERTONGUE
We're birds of a feather, we two.
TEREUS
Howso?
SILVERTONGUE
Well, I'd like to go... to a place where the worst that can happen
is a chat in the street, when I happen to meet
the father of some strapping young lad...
who then dresses me down... with some highly agreeable accusation,
saying "Some smooth-talker you are," and that he thinks I'm a cad
in that I let his son pass... without even the slightest molestation...
He'll say that I saw him, you know, on the way home from the gym...
fresh from the bath, but that I avoided his path,
and let him go by without patting his arse
– or even looking to tickle his grapes!
TEREUS
Oh you poor fellow, loving evils of that kind,
but there is a city– and well-endowed –
just of the sort... for you... It's by the Red Sea.
SILVERTONGUE
The Red Sea? – No, no, that's not a colour for me!
Besdies, the Athenians are well-endowed too, and have a fleet
of masts ready to serve summons on any foreign port...
Don't you have something Greek in your beak?
TEREUS
Well, you could seek... hmm, what about a berth then...
somewhere in Crete?
GREENHORN
No, I don't think it wise for us to become cretins.
Isn't there somewhere else we could go?
TEREUS
Well, what about the islands? Moros and Lesbos are nice.

GREENHORN

Well, that's moros or lesbos the same thing: I wouldn't want
to become a moron, nor a lesbian – not at any price... But tell me,
O Not-so-little-birdy: What's life like, then, with the birds?

TEREUS

Well, it's not actually, as they say, all just for the birds:
for starters, there's absolutely no need to carry purses...

GREENHORN

Well, that's a saving on one of life's great curses...

TEREUS

And we enter gardens with no "beg pardons", and graze
free as birds, on myrtle-berry and mint,
and on poppy and sesame seed...

GREENHORN

Well, happy days! Why your life's just one great big garden party!

TEREUS

Indeed!

SILVERTONGUE

Oho! Why, yes, that's right... you come and go as you please...
But you know, as I see it, you're wasting that great power...

TEREUS

What power?

SILVERTONGUE

The power of flight!

TEREUS

Why, what do you think we should be doing?

SILVERTONGUE

Well, for starters, you could stop flying all aflutter, like birdbrains,
with all that flocking about – and then you could stop strewing
your scratchings all over the place... You know what it means
when someone's a little too flighty... But if you could get the birds
of all feather to all flock in together, you could build up a kingdom
well, I think, er... quite high and mighty!

TEREUS
Oh, I see: flocking in – not out and about – well, that you're right,
I don't doubt it... but it sounds to me far easier said than done.
How could we possibly go about it?
SILVERTONGUE
Well, you could do the Athenian thing, like he and I are out to do...
and bringing everybody in, build yourself a city –
...but you – since of course you know how to fly –
would be best advised to build your city... in the sky!
TEREUS
A city in the sky? Hmm, I think you may be aiming far too high...
SILVERTONGUE (POINTING)
Not at all: Look down here!
TEREUS
I see.
SILVERTONGUE
Now look up!
TEREUS
I see.
SILVERTONGUE
Now twist your neck around.
TEREUS
Oh, good grief!
SILVERTONGUE
What is it?
TEREUS
I think I've broken my neck.
(REPOSITIONS HIS HEADGEAR) *Oh, that's a relief!*
SILVERTONGUE
Well, what did you see?
TEREUS
Well, I'm seeing stars, would you believe...

SILVERTONGUE
Exactly! With a little effort, there's no limit to what you can achieve.
TEREUS
I see: the sky's the limit, as they say. But let a bird enquire:
How do we build a city?
SILVERTONGUE
No, not just a city – you can build an empire!
– You looked up and saw heaven, and down and saw earth,
but t'was you stood perched here in between them...
You see, the city of birds shall be the portal 'twixt heaven and earth:
You shall rule over men like a cock on a hen,
and even the gods will come begging like you've never seen them!
TEREUS
The gods will come begging?
SILVERTONGUE
Oh yes, you see... whenever we wish to go to Delphi
– to fetch a vital piece of advice –
we must first beg safe passage of the Boeotians,
and pay them their asking price... and so it shall be,
whenever men burn offerings to the immortals... you
will be in a position to stop the aroma of the sacrifice
from wafting through your city portals! – Why,
unless the gods pay you a little tribute... a little excise
to let it through, you could starve them out...
with an aerial blockade!
TEREUS
Wha-ho! By earth, by traps, by mist-like fine-mesh-nets,
that's the most cultivated plan, by bird or man,
I've ever heard been made! I should like to found this city with you –
if the other birds are in agreement. We rule by consensus, you know.
SILVERTONGUE
But can they be convinced?

◇◈◈◈ TEREUS SUMMONS THE BIRDS ◈◈◈◇

TEREUS
I'm sure you can do it! Leastwise, have a go: for though
they are barbarians, I have taught them a few key words...
you know: having been among them so long.
SILVERTONGUE
But how can we get them all together?
TEREUS
Easy! – With a song!
I'll just have to duck back in (ahem!) and waken my songstress,
she and I shall call them: the blended harmony will do the trick;
they'll have no choice... for it's quite impossible, you know,
to resist my nightingale's voice.
SILVERTONGUE
O Dear Birdy, don't just stand there: get thee to thy nest!
Get thee 'to thy thicket... and wake-up thy songstréss!

TEREUS (EXITS INTO THE TICKET, AND IS HEARD WITHIN)
Come, my consort, leave off thy sleep,
and let loose the measures of the sacred songs,
thus with divine melody let us bewail
our long lost child... the one for whom we weep:
Trill the holy strain with jaws awarble,
let it permeate the foliage of the oak,
and with thy throat, a pure tremolo,
let it echo to Zeus's seat...
and there the golden-haired Apollo,
in hearing thy lament, will strum along
on an ivory-inlaid lyre... as if 'twere heaven sent –
and thus, with the chorus brought to its feet,
our harmonies the immortals will inspire,
in unison with the sacred music of thy song.
(HE APPEARS ON THE "BALCONY" OF THE OAK TREE ABOVE THE THICKET)

GREENHORN
O lord Zeus, what a voice on that bird!
Even solo it spreads honey through the entire grove.

A NIGHTINGALE APPEARS ON THE BALCONY AND BEGINS TO PIPE HER PART ON A FLUTE

SILVERTONGUE
Hoy!
GREENHORN
What is it?
SILVERTONGUE
Be quiet!
GREENHORN
What for?
SILVERTONGUE
Hoopoe's about to sing encore.
TEREUS (SINGS IN HARMONY WITH THE FLUTE)
Epopo-poi! Popo-popoi! Popoi!
Hoy! Hoy! Hie! Hie! Hie! Hie!
Hie-ther all ye birds of fellow feather:
all ye who take a share of the well-sown fields,
those who help themselves to the grainy yields –
Ye tribes numberless of seed-poaching race,
who dart about then fly apace,
whose dainty twitter in furrowed clods of earth,
with streams of chirrups betray your mirth:
Tio tio-tio-tio tio tio-tio-tio!
And all of you who live in gardens,
nestled among the ivy sprigs,
and ye of the mountains one-and-all,
who munch on wild cherries... and on figs,
and even those who eat the bristle-berries:
Hurry! flying to my call:

◇◈◈◈ TEREUS SUMMONS THE BIRDS ◈◈◈◇

Trioto trioto totobrix!
All who, in swamps, on boggy ground,
go after gnats and gulp them down,
with beaks oh so sharp and long,
and who inhabit earth all drenched and sodden,
wet and wild and never trodden;
birds of song... and coloured wings,
and goosey, goosey gos-e-lings!
Come hither, hither to learn the news!
Ye too, who over the swelling sea,
ye fisher-birds of flighty breed:
A clever bird has come our way...
we're cock-a-hoop – he's an entrepreneurd! –
Just come and hear ye, hear ye what he has to say!
All muster here, all fly the coop!
Yes, even us bigguns with long gangly-necks...
Hither, hither, hither, hither!
Toro-toro-toro-toro-tix.
Kikkabau, kikkabau.
Toro-toro-toro li-li-lix.

TEREUS AND THE NIGHTINGALE RETIRE

SILVERTONGUE
Do you see any birds?
GREENHORN
By Apollo, not one, none... nix –
even though I'm busting my balls to see – my eyeballs!
SILVERTONGUE
In vain from his perch, like a hen without chicks
went the hoopoe's calls...
TEREUS (RE-EMERGES, IN PANOPLY, FROM THE THICKET)
Torotix torotix.

GREENHORN
O man, but wait: there's something actually coming this way!

VARIOUS BIRDS — MEMBERS OF THE CHORUS— BEGIN TO ENTER, SEVERALLY

SILVERTONGUE
By Zeus, you're right! And it looks like a bird!
But what sort of bird is that?
GREENHORN
Maybe the man himself will say
O Tereus, what sort of bird is that?
TEREUS
That's the sort of bird you don't see every day:
it's a Dionysian-duck.
GREENHORN
Well, what the... like a flaming Phoenix!
TEREUS
Ah, you're flaming correct: that's why it's called the Flame-ingo.
GREENHORN
Oh hey: get this!
SILVERTONGUE
Why are you squawking?
GREENHORN
Here's another strange-looking bird.
SILVERTONGUE
By Zeus! This one is strange, and he casts an unhomenly aspersion.
What then is this absurd... this prophetic-looking bird?
TEREUS
Why, that one's called a Persian.
SILVERTONGUE
A Persian? O lord Herakles!
But how is it that a Persian flew in without a carpet?
GREENHORN
Hey, here's another bird with a crestfallen crown.

SILVERTONGUE
Ho-ho! Hoopoe, what's this featherless... this fallen-down, er...
wonder? You're not the only hoopoe then, for yonder...
is yet another one come to town!
TEREUS
That one belongs to Euripides, hence the pathetic plume.
But we're birds of a feather, we just don't flock together.
SILVERTONGUE
Oh, and I see he's inherited your old costume!
GREENHORN
So that's why he looks so thoroughly plucked!
TEREUS
No, that's because he's a blue-eyed boy: the shysters find him gullible,
and the females find him lovable: they souvenir his fluff, you know,
after they've been thoroughly ...
SILVERTONGUE
O Poseidon, here's yet another mottled bird!
What name does this one flutter by then?
TEREUS
Oh, he's a Fatbellybird.
GREENHORN
What? Does Kleonymos have a double too?
SILVERTONGUE
No, if he were a Kleonymos, he'd be a yellowbellybird...
or something synonymous!
GREENHORN
But why do all these birds have crests? It all looks rather Spartan.
TEREUS
No, it's more a matter of in-flight stability: you see,
the head of each family bears a crest... just like a family tartan...
as a sort of rallying point for all the rest.
SILVERTONGUE
O Poseidon, the stage is teeming with birds!

Take a look at these things!
GREENHORN
O lord Apollo, look at what? It's all awhir!
I can't even see the wings… for the wings!
TEREUS
Here's a pidgeon, and by god! there's a godwit!
And there's a duck, and there's a crane…
SILVERTONGUE
What's that one doing all that squawking? It sounds insane!
TEREUS
What else? That's a Tattletail.
GREENHORN
Is a Tattletail really a bird?
TEREUS
Of course, Athens is full of tattletales! – or so I've heard…
And there's the Athenian Owl herself!
SILVERTONGUE
Is that really wise: an owl by day?
TEREUS
Well, we couldn't get her any other way…
er, any other wise… er… anyway… anywise here's the hoarder,
hunter, diver, hawk… the cuckoo, redfoot, redcap, stork…
the swimming swan, the laying goose, the calling-bird,
and French the hen… turtledove, partridge…
SILVERTONGUE
All we need now is a pear tree, then…

THE BIRDS OF THE CHORUS ARE NOW ALL ONSTAGE,
AND DANCING IN A WILD CIRCLE, CENTRED ON THE TWO MEN

GREENHORN
Whoa woah, it's all a little scary!
SILVERTONGUE
Scary? Well, you can say that again: I feel like we're in a cage

of feathers and beaks, and birds in a rage... oh!

THE DANCING CONTINUES AWHILE, BUT ENDS WITH THE TWO MEN SURROUNDED BY A RING OF BIRDS. THE LEADER OF THE CHORUS IS OUTSIDE THE RING.

CHORUS LEADER
How-ow-ow-ow-ow-ow-ow-ow-ow-ow strange!
Where is he who called? And what's the occasion
for getting us out on stage?
TEREUS
Here I am, and when a friend's in need, I'm never out of range!
CHORUS LEADER
Wha-wha-wha-wha-wha-wha-wha-what have you got for us then?
What's on the agenda?
TEREUS
Oh, public safety, justice, benefaction, service...
and a couple of human guest speakers... with items for referenda.

A FEW OF THE BIRDS IN THE CHORUS DEFECATE AT THE MENTION OF HUMANS, AND ARE VISIBLY CONCERNED

CHORUS LEADER
What? How? When? Er... fly that one by me again...
TEREUS
I said, or should say, that two venerables have come this way
here from the world-of-men, concerning matters of great importance.

SEVERAL OTHER BIRDS DEFECATE, OR FART, AT THE MENTION OF MEN

CHORUS LEADER
Oh, is that a rotten egg I smell brewing?
You shouldn't even joke like that: It could be my undoing!
TEREUS
No need to get your feathers in a flap!
CHORUS LEADER
But what's going on then?

TEREUS
Well, under my wing... I have taken two men
with hearts that beat like those of birds.
CHORUS LEADER
But what business are they in?
TEREUS
They're looking to feather their own nests, no doubt –
just like me and you.
CHORUS LEADER
And you have taken them in?
TEREUS
Why not? They're as much like you as I... They're one of us,
though they don't fly, and there's not actually one, but two!
CHORUS LEADER
Not naturalized?
TEREUS
Yes, fully fledged!
CHORUS
Oh! Suffering sacrileged! – He's sold us out!
He's become the quisling cuckoo in the nest...
the snake in the undergrowth... the ancient laws transgressed!
He's broken his avian oath! – He took communion with us,
and flocked with us in the meadow... but now he's hung us out
before that unholy race... the very one that has ever been
our mortal foe... the one we're always dreading!
CHORUS LEADER
Well, let's postpone his case... we can settle accounts with him later:
but it seems to me... that these intruders... well, they can be got, er...
served a little summary justice here on the spot!
Time to do some shredding!

THE BIRDS OF THE CHORUS STRETCH THEIR WINGS MENACINGLY
AND BEGIN TO ENCIRCLE THE TWO MEN

SILVERTONGUE
Hey, this is not... exactly what I had in mind.
GREENHORN
I must have been out of my mind to follow you here.
And for what?
SILVERTONGUE
Well, every leader needs a follower, you know: to cover his behind.
GREENHORN
You mean: so that I... could cry a lot.
SILVERTONGUE
Don't get delerious: how could you cry
once they've pecked out your eyes?
CHORUS LEADER
View halloo! Advance! Attack! Let's get these two!
Bring in both wings! Close the circle! Keep them in the ring!
This pair must learn to sing... and furnish fodder for my beak!
There's no lofty cloud, no mountain peak, no churning sea
that will receive this pair in flight from me!
CHORUS (BEGINNING TO ENCIRCLE THE MEN IN A MENACING DANCE)
So let's not wait, let no-one hesitate...
to peck these two, nor pluck'em!
GREENHORN
This is it... Oh, woe is me!
CHORUS LEADER
Where's the lieutenant? Have him bring the right wing 'round.
GREENHORN
To where can I flee?
SILVERTONGUE
You there, hold your ground!
GREENHORN
But we can't just stand here all day, trying to dodge and duck'em!
SILVERTONGUE
But how do you think to get away?

GREENHORN
I have no clue.
SILVERTONGUE
Well, I'll tell you what to do: We need to stand and fight!
that's what: If we can keep the owls at bay, we can get away
in the middle of the night! – Here, grab this pot!
GREENHORN
What good's a pot?
SILVERTONGUE
Use your head, man: put it on! It'll protect you when they swoop...

A SALVO OF DROPPINGS FLIES OVERHEAD

...and poop.
GREENHORN
Oh, and we'll look like a couple of old peace-pots too!

THEY DON THE POTS, AS HELMETS

But what about the threat of ground attack?
SILVERTONGUE
Ah, just grab a skewer... then plant-it-fast in front of you.
And there: a palisade! And here's another to cover your back!
GREENHORN
But what about our eyes?
SILVERTONGUE
Well, just take out a cup... or two, and cover up!
GREENHORN (HOLDING CUPS TO HIS EYES, AS IF THEY WERE BINOCULARS)
O you're the cleverest! In generalship you win the prize:
You've done so well in coming-up with things to use...
Why, you've already out-boobied Nikias... in the siege of Syracuse.
CHORUS LEADER
Gra-gra-grab'em! Move out! Lower your beaks!
Don't hold back! Peck'em! Pluck'em! Draw and quarter'em!
And take the skin off too! (ASIDE:) I hate the skin.

TEREUS
Tell me, you: leader of this motley crew,
why are you aiming to slaughter'em,
these men, who have clearly done nought to you?
Besides, they're related to my wife: her kith 'n' kin...
CHORUS LEADER
Oh, they're in-laws of yours... and you still want to spare them?
Are you sure?
TEREUS
These two I do... This pair have come here with this great idea
that they're willing to share... with you.
CHORUS LEADER
But has there ever been a human who wouldn't catch or kill a bird?
TEREUS
Why, that's absurd: just take a look. (HE POINTS AT THE TWO MEN, WHOSE HELMETS RESEMBLE EGGSHELLS) Why, these men look more like
doves, or even cute hatchling chicks...
CHORUS LEADER
Hmm, to me, they look like a couple of pr-pr-pr...
ne'er-do-well pr-pr-professors!
TEREUS
Pr-pr-precisely! and they've come here ready, willing, and able
to teach us something handy.
CHORUS LEADER
Handy? Well, if you've got hands, I suppose that's dandy!
But how could we ever learn anything from a race of such arrant
aggressors? Why, they've been our enemies from time immemorial.
TEREUS
But what if they're enemies by birth, yet friends by intent?
Besides, not every lesson is taught by a friend.
Take "Caution", for instance, as the number one tutorial:
it often saves the day... but that's a lesson that, in the end,
a wise bird can only learn, in a way... from an enemy!

Why, 'twas foes, not friends, that first drove men
to construction of mighty walls, and fighting ships:
and that safeguards hearth and home, and kith and kin...
why, 'twas invaluable instruction...

CHORUS LEADER
Alright then, Stand down! – It may indeed be the wise bird who...
will hear what they have to say.

THE BIRDS OF THE CHORUS STOP THEIR MENACING DANCE

SILVERTONGUE
It seems like their anger is on the ebb.
Look! Look! Fall back, eyes-front!

TEREUS
And it's really just the right thing to do...

CHORUS LEADER
Well, we do tend to bow... to anyone who wears a crown.
(HE BOWS TO TEREUS)

GREENHORN
They're acting more peaceable, by Zeus!
Perhaps you haven't cooked our goose...

SILVERTONGUE
Ahem. (AS IF BARKING ORDERS) *Pots and cups: Let... down!*
But let us shoulder the skewer, men, and keep the watch,
and have our pots at the ready: Gentlemen, we must die or do!

GREENHORN
But if we do actually die, where on earth will they bury us?

SILVERTONGUE
They shall ferry us – our bones – to Potter's Field...
for some stranger shall go tell the Athenians our famous last words:
"We refuse to yield!" and that we held our ground – and pots –
and flew not from the birds.

CHORUS LEADER
Reform ranks! Stand at ease: and like soldiers doffing your armour,

leave your rage and anger behind.
Let's find out who these men may be, and where they're from,
and what they have in mind.
(THERE'S A LONG PAUSE)
Hoy, Hoopoe, that's your cue.

TEREUS

My cue for what?

CHORUS LEADER

Not for what, for who! Who are these two,
and are they coming or going?

TEREUS

They're a couple of wise old owls, from Athens.

CHORUS LEADER

What chance then – what circumstance then –
has them gone... er, come to the birds?

TEREUS

Why, they love birdlife and all manner of feather...
and they want to be one of us, and to live with us all,
and to have us all live as one... together.

CHORUS LEADER

What are you saying? What sort of story are they telling?

TEREUS

Unbelievable it is, unheard-of, and beyond.

CHORUS LEADER

But are they just sniffing about, hoping to feather
their own nests with this story that they're selling?
Or maybe just scratching 'round, laying the ground,
hoping to put one over on their enemies...
or maybe just a leg up to their friends?

TEREUS

Well, their leader's talking big things: incredible,
inexpressable prosperity, undreamt-of dividends...
He says we're looking at the prospect of having it all:

here, there, and everywhere we go.
CHORUS LEADER
Is he ranting or raving, or what?
TEREUS
Well, there's a fine line between genius and insanity, you know.
CHORUS LEADER
Well, which side is he on?
TEREUS
Well, he's as cunning as a fox, as shifty as a rat,
and as clever as a crow... He's as slippery as a snake,
and as agile as a cat... and for all of that, you know,
I'd say he's not a nutter.
CHORUS LEADER
Well, tell him to speak up, for goodness' sake.
For even just hearing what you've said so far...
has me all aflutter!
TEREUS (TO TWO SLAVEBIRDS AS HE DOFFS HIS PANOPLY)
Come then, you and you: take this back inside,
and hang it up for good – all things going well – in the kitchen,
by the fire, behind the firewood. (TO SILVERTONGUE) *And you...*
you need now to make the speech that I called them in to hear:
and you'd better make it good... or we'll both be hanging out to dry.
SILVERTONGUE
No, I shall not... No, by Apollo, not I... Not unless they give to me
a guarantee like the monkey got... from his overbirdlike wife...
when she swore not to snip at his what's-it, nor to slash
at his thingies, with her beak-like carving knife.
CHORUS LEADER
You don't mean his... hem (COVERS HIS GROIN) *and his, er...*
(COVERS HIS BOTTOM) *behind, I hope?*
SILVERTONGUE
Nope! 'twas ours I had in mind – and no pecking at the eyes!

CHORUS LEADER
You have our word.
SILVERTONGUE
Then let's hear it now.
CHORUS LEADER
We swear on this condition: that our play this day
– in this here competition... by unanimous vote
of all the judges – be awarded absolute first prize!
SILVERTONGUE
Oh, it shall be so!
CHORUS LEADER
But if we should overstep the mark, or sing a note
in praise of the honourable author: a victory by just one vote!
TEREUS (TO THE CHORUS)
Listen, folks: the raptors can now get their weapons up, ahem...
and back home you all can go... but be keeping an eye out
in case we post an update on the noticeboard.
CHORUS
Treacherous always and in every way is man begot:
but all the same, before we fly-out... we'll hear what you have to say.
Perhaps you're going to reveal something magic that you've seen in us,
some untapped power, some exposé... of something we've overlooked,
something for which our brains were just too small...
So spit-it-out! and share the love, don't keep it under wraps,
For if you come up with the goods, it'll benefit one-and-all!
CHORUS LEADER
That's right: don't hold back, and be not afearing,
we'll hold our peace til you've had a hearing.
So spin your yarn: we're all ears... Try to turn
our heads now – with your big ideas!
SILVERTONGUE
By Zeus, I've got it all worked-up and ready to spout,
and now there's nothing to stop it being spurted out:

Quick! Someone fetch me a napkin, and get me some water
to wash my hands!

GREENHORN

Are we getting ready for dinner? Or what?

SILVERTONGUE

No, by Zeus, we're not... that's just to wipe 'em off and cool 'em,
coz I'm boiling-over with such red-hot tales of things
to tantalize these birds... (ASIDE:) *...and to maybe even fool 'em!*
(TO THE BIRDS:) *Thus I grieve for you, who once were kings –*

CHORUS LEADER

We were kings? Of what lands?

SILVERTONGUE

Why, of everything! Of all there is... of me for starters,
and of this man too... and of Zeus. Why, the birds were born
before old Father Time... and even before old Mother... Earth!

CHORUS LEADER

Before Earth?

SILVERTONGUE

Yes, by Apollo!

CHORUS LEADER

By Zeus, I had never heard of that.

SILVERTONGUE

Well, ignorance is not a crime... but if you'd studied your Aesop,
you'd know that the lark was born long before Earth,
since – when she was looking to build her nest – for dearth
of earth, she had to settle 'pon a cloud, up there in the sky...

GREENHORN

Skylarking then?

SILVERTONGUE

No, this is serious: since she was born before Mother Earth...
then that's proof that every bird... is a prince,
that the birds are older than the Titans and the gods
– you know: Zeus, and all the rest... and by right of primal birth...

'tis they should rule the n... roost...
GREENHORN
Good god then! So it really does pay... to be an early bird –
but say: won't Zeus be a little reluctant
to swap his sceptre with a woodcock? (Ahem!)
SILVERTONGUE
Ah, but since the past is prologue, as they say,
let me give my case a boost... for the birds ruled men
in olden days... and here now I give the proof: Exhibit A...
(A ROOSTER STEPS FORWARD FROM THE CHORUS) *...the common cock!*
Often called the Persian bird... for once he ruled
in the land of the cocked headsock, that beanie-bonnet so absurd...
long before the great king Darius, and that bigmouth Megaword.
GREENHORN
Is that why the cock struts around like the Great King even now,
alone of those with feathers... crowned with a coxcomb on his head?
SILVERTONGUE
Yes, and his powers are in no way diminished, I'll have you know,
for to this day, before the dawn, he has but to crow...
and everyone's up and out of bed:
coppersmiths, cobblers, tanners of leathers...
butchers, bakers, even candlestick makers... and they're off to work,
in the dark, before they even get their boot-straps on.
GREENHORN
I can vouch for that, for I, poor jerk...
lost a cape of Phrygian wool
because of some cock without a friggian clock:
I was in town at the time, for the naming of a newborn niece,
and I'd had one or two... well, I'd had a few,
and was thinking to take a little nap before the feast...
The sun had just settled, and so had I – passed out on the lawn –
when this cock up and crowed... and I naturally took it for the dawn...
well, I thought I'd missed the whole darn thing,

and had best, well, hit the road...
so there I am, just ducking out past the big-city-walls
when a snatcher lets me have it – with a club in the balls –
and before I could even croak, the bastard had got away...
and made off with my cloak.

SILVERTONGUE

As I was saying, way back in the day, 'twas the kite that held sway...
why, he lorded it even over the Greeks...

CHORUS LEADER

Over the Greeks?

SILVERTONGUE

...and under his wing they learned how to pray,
by using their hands to make themselves beaks,
and he showed them how to dive to the ground
when they pray... and to hover...

GREENHORN

Yes, well the kite is a bird of prey, as they say,
and, you know, I dropped to my knees once on seeing a kite,
as I thought it some peculiar alms-begging right...
so there I am, hovering, with my hands in a bundle...
but, to dive south, I had to pop all my pennies up into my mouth...
It all sounds hard to swallow I know, but what's worse,
I went home that day... with nothing but sore knees –
and a great empty purse!

SILVERTONGUE

And furthermore, the cuckoo...
was king over the Egyptian and the Jew...
and whenever he clucked "Cook! Cock!",
some would scramble in search of eggs to poach,
others some grains would mow... and yet others would get all hot
and horny sowing wild oats – and not just with a hoe!

GREENHORN

So the proverb is true of the cuckoo too:

"Even with the skin cut off the cuckoo's cock,
it'll go out and pl(a)y the field."
SILVERTONGUE
And if ever there were an Agamemnon
or Menelaos, or other human king...
a bird would sit 'pon his sceptre or his shield...
and share in the gifts that other men might bring.
GREENHORN
Well, that's something else I'd never heard,
but that explains why – in the tragedies –
why the king Priams always come out with a bird...
Why else would they be set there, but to keep an eye
on the bribes... the tragic judges all get fed!
SILVERTONGUE
But the most impressive proof of all is that Zeus,
the current king, has an eagle on his head –
as an emblem of his royal blood, that is –
and his daughter too, an owl; and Apollo, too,
upon his arm – as 'twere his right-hand-man... a hawk.
GREENHORN
Yes, by Demeter, and that's convincing talk,
but on what account do they have them?
SILVERTONGUE
Why? – So that whenever someone making a sacrifice
holds the innards high... they can snatch them in advance –
for Zeus, that is – before any other god even has half a chance...
And nowadays, when they're up to no good,
you'll hear the priests swear their oaths "by goose"
– as if they're just mispronouncing Zeus –
or somehow lost for words...
But in the old days nobody would swear by a god at all,
but everyone – by birds! (HE TURNS TO THE BIRDS:)
Yes, everyone once honoured you as high and holy,

but now your stocks are low... people think you're simple,
birdbrains, maniacs... and everywhere you go –
even in sanctuaries – they throw
things at you, like you've got targets on your backs...
and every birdhunter, why, they're out to get you,
out to put a few new feathers in their caps...
they set snares, and nooses, nebula, nets,
and even sticky twigs for traps...
then they sell you at the market,
and shoppers give your flesh a squeeze...
and if you're nice and plump they take you home
and have you roasted, but not content to stop at that,
no: they grate up a little cheese...
and add a little oil, some silphium, vinegar...
then they rub it in... But wait! here comes another basting,
with hot sauces, savory and sweet...
and on it goes, still boiling – scalding – as if you were dead-meat!

CHORUS
That's the uttermost, most grievous speech, human,
that yet here thou hast brought.
How we bemoan the failings of our fathers,
from whom we inherit – nought:
Who came unstuck in passing those honours
of our forefathers on from theirs...
CHORUS LEADER
But thou, by some spirit and happenstance benevolent,
thou hast come to us as saviour.
So now we bequeath to thee the ministry
over our nestlings... and of our domestic and foreign affairs!
CHORUS
Yes, we want our kingdom back, for heaven's sakes...
Why, life isn't worth living without it –

and you are obviously here to teach us what has to be done...
So tell us and we'll do it – whatever it takes!
SILVERTONGUE
In that case, Lesson One:
there should be one great-big-sky-high city of birds,
consolidated... with the sky surrounded all about
by a great wall of kiln-dried bricks, just like Babylon.
TEREUS
O Gog and Magog, what a fortress that would be!
SILVERTONGUE
Yes, never to be impregnated!
And when this has been erected against him...
demand the primacy back from Zeus:
and if he doesn't agree, or seems unwilling,
a holy war must be effected against him!
Forbid of the gods that they cum and go
through your passages, all erect the way they do –
you know how they've been going down, oh so clever,
and knocking-up human victims since forever – and even before...
and if they keep on trying to penetrate these forbidden areas,
set your royal seal upon their their knobs – stitch 'em up –
so that they can't fuck those poor women anymore!
To the humans, however... I urge you send out a herald
with this report... proclaiming the primacy of the birds,
and that sacrifices henceforth be firstly unto you –
and only to the gods as an afterthought.
And let it be known, by all mankind... that to each of the gods
a suitable bird be assigned... one right, proper, and fit... so that,
for instance, those sacrificing to Aphrodite,
must think firstly of the tit... but if it's a sheep to Poseidon –
your sacrifice – then some sardines to the gull, I think would be nice...
And if it's a beast to that glutton Herakles,
nothing short of your entire feast – to the pelican – will suffice.

GREENHORN
... whose beak holds more than his...
SILVERTONGUE
Yes, yes...
GREENHORN
And to Zeus... the king?
SILVERTONGUE
Well, to the cock of the roost? Hmm, I think an uncastrated gadfly
would be just the thing.
GREENHORN
A gadfly? Oh, a gnat! Why, that's a sacrifice I'd be happy to bring.
And let's hear the great Zeus thunder at that!
CHORUS LEADER
But how will they take us for gods and not poppinjays,
we who flit about and have wings?
SILVERTONGUE
Oh, don't be so stupid... Why, Hermes's a god with wings on his feet...
and his hat! And Victory, too, gets about with wings of gold...
and so does Cupid... and, according to Homer, Iris is like a flighty dove.
CHORUS LEADER
That may be, but won't Zeus try to compete...
with thunderbolts winging our way from the heavens above?
SILVERTONGUE
Piss and wind! – Why, if through ignorance and zeal
men still believe you to be nothing, and that those in Olympus are real,
then let a cloud of sparrows be raised, and nit-pickers sent down
to devour their seed in the field! And then, when they're famished,
let them see what she of the crops... what Demeter is willing to yield.
GREENHORN
Mother Nature? But she's notoriously fickle.
SILVERTONGUE
And to drive the point home, as they roll out their ploughs,
send down some crows: their beaks are hooked, to this end,

as you know, like a sickle... and then swooping low,
let's have the blood flow... as they peck the eyes right out of their cows!
GREENHORN
Oooh!
SILVERTONGUE
Oh, and then let Apollo... put them back in,
since he's the heavenly Healer: he's been drawing wages
for things like this, now, for ages...
GREENHORN
In that case, hold off... until my heifers can be sold off.
SILVERTONGUE (TO THE BIRDS)
But if they follow you as their Zeus, their Earth, their Poseidon,
that is, ahem, as their gods of seas and lands and airs... why,
that's a virtual guarantee that good things always... will be theirs.
TEREUS
How good?
SILVERTONGUE
Well, for starters, locusts will no longer devour their vine stalks...
they'll be wiped out by a flying squad – of owls and hawks.
Nor shall gallbugs and mites be forever destroying the fig and the bean:
a task-force of thrushes shall round them all up – sweep them all clean...
CHORUS LEADER
But how shall we give men wealth? That's what they really want.
SILVERTONGUE
Well, you know how men love to read the omens of birds
when their fortunes they seek... Well the bird under consultation
shall simply have to open his beak... to spill his guts to the augur,
to sing like a bird, so to speak... Not like now, where birdsong to men...
GREENHORN
...well, to them it's all Greek!
SILVERTONGUE
Precisely: no more oracular doublespeak... No man at the helm
shall ever again, er... end up, er...

GREENHORN
...up shit creek?
SILVERTONGUE
No, there'll always be a bird about to offer a pre-voyage tip...
like "Don't sail now, there's going to be a storm",
or "sail now, there's profit in the wind".
GREENHORN
Profit in the wind? In that case... (HE FARTS)
...I think I'll get myself a ship, and become a merchant-man.
SILVERTONGUE
And birds shall point out treasures – full of coins – that men
of old have hidden... for you know, they've had a bird's-eye-view
of everything, even secrets long forbidden.
TEREUS
So that's why people are wont to say: "no one knew
where my treasure lay, till a little birdy told me"?
GREENHORN
Well, I'm selling the ship, getting a spade,
and heading off to dig up some beaches.
CHORUS LEADER
But how will they give men health? That's still in the hands
of the gods, and that's worth more than wealth.
SILVERTONGUE
Ah, your grasp of cause and effect I believe is suspect,
for have you ever seen a pauper who was healthy?
But if you turn it around, a man whose body is sound...
is quite invariably wealthy!
CHORUS LEADER
But what about old age then? A man's days too,
are numbered by Zeus: or will the good still die, as now they do...
in the cradle?
SILVERTONGUE
No, by god! The stork shall deliver three-hundred years, and more!

CHORUS LEADER
From where?
SILVERTONGUE
From where? Why, from the flock, they have it in stock,
don't you know... for t'was Hesiod said "five generations of men...
is the span of the squawking crow"?
GREENHORN
Aha! So much better than Zeus to have these birds on the throne!
SILVERTONGUE
So much so! – For starters, we shan't have to build temples in stone
just to house them, nor to shut them in with gates of gold as well,
but in treetops, not temples, under copses and oaklets, they shall dwell...
And the olive branch shall be temple to even the most majestic
of the birds, nor shall we have to go to Delphi,
nor to kneel and mouth exotic words, for we shall stand...
among the wild-olives and the strawberry-trees,
holding barley and wheat in an outstretched hand...
as we pray for a little share of blessings, and these...
shall be tossed off to us – ungrudgingly – for just the cost...
of us having tossed... to them... a little seed.
CHORUS LEADER
O, from our most hated foe transformed – to a friend indeed!
How could we ever think of failing you now!
CHORUS
Exulting in these thy words... we take on oath and forewarn of how...
if you lay fair-minded plans before us... and honest undertakings
against the gods... singing mutual thoughts in harmony with our chorus...
we shall soon be pounding those mere immortals
– with our newly roused-up rods!
CHORUS LEADER
And in whatever requires the use of force
– or the application of brawn:
why, we shall be disposed to do it...

but in anything requiring deliberation – or brains, of course –
that shall be laid upon you – for we eschew it.
TEREUS
Well then, by Zeus, let's not be caught napping,
nor thinking to win victory by delay...
come on in to this nest of mine
– one of our more humble productions, you know:
just sticks and hay – and we'll get to the introductions.
Er...
SILVERTONGUE
Yes?
TEREUS
Er... you have me at something of a disadvantage, gentlemen...
SILVERTONGUE
Yes?
TEREUS
Er, your names...?
SILVERTONGUE
Oh! Our names: Well, that bit's easy: people call me Silvertongue,
but I'm Buddy to every friend.
TEREUS
Good-o, and you...?
GREENHORN
'Ripideasy.
SILVERTONGUE
Commonly known as Greenhorn.
TEREUS
I see. Good, then, gentlemen: Welcome. Now let's ascend!
GREENHORN (TO SILVERTONGUE:) *Ascend?*

TEREUS FLIES UP ONTO THE BALCONY

SILVERTONGUE
Hold it! A glitch! Back-up here – (or down) – all oars astern!

I think I may have spotted a tiny problem, a minor detail,
of course, but a cause of some concern...
TEREUS (RETURNING)
Well, what is it?
SILVERTONGUE
Well, you may recall how in Aesop... there's that fable...
about the eagle and the fox?
TEREUS
Yes...?
SILVERTONGUE
...and how they made that deal...?
TEREUS
Yes...?
SILVERTONGUE
And how, because the eagle could fly, but the fox was unable...
he ended up feeding her cubs... to his chicks...?
TEREUS
Yes...?
GREENHORN
... but how the fox got even when she...
SILVERTONGUE (TO GREENHORN:)
Nix, nix... (TO TEREUS:) *...er, we won't go into detail right now,*
but the problem is this: How... are we going to manage
this little marriage of ours, when you can fly, but we... er...
TEREUS
Oh, never mind that: there's a particular root, you know,
it does wonders for the wings: in fact, if you eat it raw,
you'll soon be flying... but in the meantime you can use the door...
SILVERTONGUE
Right-o, then, lead the way...
(TO THE SLAVES:) *Boys, grab the gear, and bring it in!*
CHORUS LEADER (TO TEREUS:)
Wait a bit, Hoopoe: a quick word...

TEREUS
Why, what is it?
CHORUS LEADER
Listen, by all means, take these men with you, and feed them up:
but that sweet-voiced songbird... won't you let her out to play?
Fetch her out here and leave her to amuse us...
we'll dance to her tune, in harmony with the Muses...
GREENHORN
Oh, do indeed, by Zeusus! Let them turn your head, Hoopoe:
flush that little birdy out...
SILVERTONGUE
Yea, pipe her out, by god: let's see what's behind that beautiful voice.
TEREUS
Well, if you insist, I have no choice... O Prokne! Honeybun!
Come on out, and give these guests – something to sing about...

PROKNE, THE NIGHTINGALE, COMES OUT OF THE THICKET.
SHE IS A FLAUTIST, AND IN A VERY REVEALING COSTUME

SILVERTONGUE
O much-revered Zeus! what a beautiful little chick.
GREENHORN
Oh, what a nice piece of fluff! With thighs like that...
SILVERTONGUE
Oh, what fun... a man could really make a cock of himself...
GREENHORN
...or a dick!
SILVERTONGUE
She looks just like a princess.
GREENHORN
I think I'd like to screw her.
SILVERTONGUE
Well, Prince Charming, be careful:

that beak's as sharp as a skewer!
GREENHORN
I'd like to think of it as a nut-cracker,
and I've got just the nuts required.
TEREUS
Ahem! Well, let's go in.
SILVERTONGUE
Lead us on, then, and may our fortunes be inspired.
(EXEUNT, INTO THE THICKET, ALL BUT PROKNE AND THE CHORUS)

CHORUS
O belovéd nightingale, sister songstress,
companion of our every hymn,
We see thee at last!
and O how sweet the melodies,
the sounds here thou dost bring!
O dearest of all the birds, thou hast come...
but now let us go: lead thee off our anapests,
pipe us the very voice of spring;
strike thee beautiful tones upon thy pipe anon –
and to thy tune now we shall sing.
CHORUS LEADER
Come ye then, ye mere men, fragile as the race of leaves,
teetering on the edge of life, wingless creatures of a day,
ye of the tribe of fleeting shadows, ye suffering mortals,
dreamlike fellows, ye of little mark, ye of feet of clay:
turn your minds to us now...
the immortal, the everlasting, the unageing, the highbrow...
er, the etherial... of the imperishable resolve,
so that you hear correctly about all things magisterial...
that to you we now shall tell...
and that knowing aright the nature of birds,
the origin of the gods and of rivers and of Heaven and Hell...

you can hereafter let Sokrates know... which way he ought to go!
Firstly there was Chaos and Night, and Erebos dark and Tartaros deep,
and there was no Heaven, nor Earth, nor Air...
but then, black-winged Night laid a wind-giving egg
in the yawning womb of darkness, and out of there...
from the upset belly of Erebos, thus aching and achurning...
was let fly Eros, egg of desire, wings all aglitter like golden fire...
not unlike a breaking wind aburning!
Better out than in, and under the cloak of black-winged Night,
with fluttering Chaos that bad egg Eros...
er, well, he did his thing... and from the bowels of Tartaros deep
he hatched up into the light... the race of things with wings.
You see, before Eros rooted everything 'round
there were actually no immortals at all to be found...
Yet crossing this with that, and up with down,
why, Heaven and Earth came into the equation
– and the Ocean – but then only later came that blesséd race
of great lofty Olympian persuasion.
Thus, you see, we are much older than all of the gods on high,
and our kinship with Eros shows in many things: Well, like him,
we fly, and we're equally indispensable to lovers on the make... Why,
many a strictly celibate lad has made it near his use-by date
– you know: manhood on his biological clock...
When bam! – that whoreson hunger seduces him to take
the gift of a goose, or a quail, from a coot... for a cock.
And mortals get help from us birds in many a practical thing...
why, by us the seasons are attested:
the time for ploughing in the spring,
the time for autumn harvest,
and the season of the sailor's winter storm:
thus for the helmsman to hibernate the tiller
when the cold takes hold,
and for that snowdropper Orestes to be arrested,

or to hang up his cloak, so as to keep us warm...
... time to grab the shears when the kite appears,
to give the sheep a trim... to sow your seed when the stork takes flight,
and yes, it's the swallow that follows him...
Springtime at last, so I suggest – as well you might...
that you sell that cloak already, you're clearly overdressed!
Yes, we are your Ammon and Delphi,
your prime oracular forecasters...
for you turn to us as you do to them – hoping to avoid disasters:
be it in travel and trade, or in a new path in life,
or even in a man's chances of finding a wife...
Yes, you esteem us decisive in anything to do with prophesy:
a bird on the right, and you're on the right track...
a bird on the left makes you wish that you hadn't – so you turn back...
When oracles speak, you say they sing "just like birds"...
and when a soothsprayer sneezes, you can see the plume of his words...
when you hear a bad plan, you say "that's not gonna fly",
and when you see vultures circling... er, well, never say die...
but is it not obvious that we are your very prognostic Apollo?
CHORUS
Since as prophets you deem us, why not as gods then esteem us,
to get the full thrust of our muse, magic, miracles and views?
CHORUS LEADER
Why, we'll bring fairwinds, and tailwinds, and rainstorms,
and such, and summers only a little bit stifling...
and you'll get gods who don't go missing in the clutch, like yon Zuse...
all aloof, and up there on the roof, head in the clouds, and trifling...
No, we'll be here with youse...
CHORUS
... giving you life, peace, youth, health,
happiness, laughter, dances, wealth...
CHORUS LEADER
... festivals! – and even bird's milk, to your children,

and to your children's children; here now, and forever ever after.
Why, you'll be so rich in everything, you'll be praying for a rest
from all those things that everyone thinks – are best!

CHORUS

O Muse of the forest,
multifarious... with whom
– tio-tio-tio-tio, tio-tio-tio-tinks –
perched in fountains of leafy throngs,
in oak and ash – tio-tio, tio-tio-tinks
on mountain peak and lowland areas,
from warbling throats and beaks like prongs
– tio-tio, tio-tio-tinks
we proclaim for Pan sacred passages
– tio-tio, tio-tio-tinks
and holy refrains for the Mountain Mother,
to whom the chorus-dance belongs
– tio-tio, tio-tio-tinks
from whence, like a bee, Pindar
ever fed upon the fruit of immortal strains,
and carried-off sweet songs –
totototototototototinks.

CHORUS LEADER

O Ladies and Gentlemen, if any of you want to wend your way
through life with an untarnished reputation... then come to us,
for everything that's disgraceful among you Athenians,
here among the birds is greeted with approbation.
Why, in Athens, as the custom stands, it's disgraceful
to strike your father... but here, if some lad takes after his dad –
and with his pecker from behind – saying "here, old cock:
watch out for your flock!" – well, among the birds
there's not a soul will mind – in fact, they'd almost wish you rather!
Or if one of you happens to have a tatoo, having run away

from your master: why, with us you're just a dappled jailbird...
but if you're a plagiarizer as tragic as Sparatos, as a bird
you can sing like a parrotos – and like him parrot Sophokles
word for word. – Or if a man's henpecked, and a wannabe citizen
like Jonah the Jew... he can cuckold himself, and be birds-of-a-feather
with all the other bustards around here; and, you know:
I'm not excluding you! – But if anyone's a nightman as hopeless
as that son of Peisias – you know: the one they call "the Nightowl"...
the one for whom no deed of a night seems far too filthy or foul...
Yes, that's the one, the son-of-a-gun who lets every vandal
under his eye pass by... Well, let's let him take flight
as a fledging barnfowl – the blaggard – since, you know,
with us, no·one sees any disgrace... in letting a "bad egg" fly!

A LOUD FART RIPPLES FROM ONE OF THE BIRDS IN THE CHORUS,
WHOSE MEMBERS TURN TO EACH OTHER WITH MURMURS OF APPROBATION

CHORUS
That's how once the swans
– tio-tio, tio-tio-tinks –
on the banks of the river Hebron,
wings aflutter in flatulent unison
– tio-tio, tio-tio-tinks –
for Apollo let fly the cry
– tio-tio, tio-tio-tinks.
Every earthly creature was taken with fright,
but that huzzah reached a mighty height,
in the upper realms of the sky...
– totototototototototinks –
...and there, in the cloudless air, it dissipated
but all of Heaven on high reverberated:
and though the Olympian lords were mystified...
the Graces and Muses sang a joyful melody in reply
– tio-tio, tio-tio, tio-tio-tinks.

CHORUS LEADER
Nothing's better than a pair of wings...
why, for you lot they'd be simply marvelous things...
For starters, when you're weighed down by all that heavy stuff
the chorus in a tragedy sings... you know: and you get a little peckish...
Well! if you had wings you could lighten things... up
– by flying off home for a snack... then, later on,
when you're as full as a boot, you could wing your way back –
and in plenty of time for the comedies!
And if one of you happens to feel a crap coming on...
you could flap your wings and become airborne...
without the risk of farting and following through, like Patrokleides,
when he shat in his own nest at last year's initiation...
No, you could fly up there and draw a breath of fresh air,
then float back down to your seat without the slightest stain
on your cloak – or even on your good reputation!
And if one of you happens to be getting a bit on the side
from a councillor's wife, and you see the kind husband
enjoying the show over there in the V.I.P. seats...
well! flap, flap! – and you're off for some more...
and there's no chance of strife, for your arse is well-covered...
(but not saying the same for the good lady),
for once having played her the whore... you can fly back here
without the slightest chance of being discovered!
So I rest my case, for as you can see,
there's nothing more desirable than that a man
sprouts a couple of good sturdy wings.
Why, just look at Dieitrephes, here: he once had no better wings
than those he used to weave onto his wicker-work bottles
– as handles, of course... but then! Well, look at him now:
he's a cavalier, with a grip on the reins of an entire battalion!
You see, his wickerwork wings have lifted him up:
he's been elevated from basket weaver to captain of a thousand men

– and horse... Yes, he's flying high: he's now a knight in shining armour:
a strutting wickerwork cockstallion!

SILVERTONGUE (ENTERS, ON THE BALCONY, AS A MOP-TOPPED BLACKBIRD)
Speaking of which! (HE FLIES DOWN FROM THE BALCONY,
FOLLOWED CLUMSILY BY GREENHORN, GOT UP LIKE A BEDRAGGLED GOOSE)
Well, I've never ever seen anything more ridiculous, by Zeus.
GREENHORN
What are you laughing at?
SILVERTONGUE
At those tail-feathers of yours: You look like a banged-up,
half-baked, part-time goose.
GREENHORN
Well, "give us the gift"... you look like you've just had a close shave
with a legal eagle, so you can't talk... an't looks like you got short shrift!
SILVERTONGUE
No, I think the barber was three-quarts barbarian.
GREENHORN
Must've been a Moe-hawk, then.
SILVERTONGUE
Barbarian, stooge: it's all the same.
TEREUS (FLIES IN)
Ahem, Gentlemen... perhaps we can now get down to business?
SILVERTONGUE
Right-o, good... well, firstly, our new city needs a name...
one grand and remarkable – without too much tizziness,
so that we can perform the dedication –
with a sacrifice to the gods, of course.
TEREUS
Most appropriate.

THERE'S A LONG PAUSE, DURING WHICH THE TRIO VISIBLY RACK THEIR BRAINS

GREENHORN
Hmm... Hey, this is harder than I thought.
How do you come up with a name out of nowhere?
TEREUS
Well, what about expropriation? – We could borrow a name
from those with some to spare... the Lakonians, for instance;
men of few words, they are, over there...
GREENHORN
Yes, why not a spare Laconic name: We could call it Spare-town?
SILVERTONGUE
Sparetown! Spare me! That's Spar-tan for snobs. "Spar-town..." No!
Would I like to couch my city in laconic terms? No! Would I like to lay
her out with Spartan seed? No! Knock her up on a Spartan couch?
No! No! No indeed! – I wouldn't be seen dead on a Spartan couch,
in Spartan trappings, or casting seed on stoney Spartan ground –
talk about pearl before the swine...
GREENHORN
Whoa, fine... Sparta farta. – What sort of name then?
TEREUS
Well, one derived from the clouds and the aetherial regions,
you know: one absoloutely mist-ifyin'.
SILVERTONGUE
Hmm... Then what about, er... Cloud-, er... -cuckoo-... hmm... -land?
TEREUS
Yo-ho, you have hit straight on it! That's a great, a beautiful name –
and uncontrived!

ALL CLEAR THEIR THROATS

GREENHORN
Cloudcuckooland... Isn't that where most of Elon's substance
is derived... and all of Donald Trump's?
SILVERTONGUE
It's actually the smoking plain of Phlegra, where the gods finally

managed to toss... those great overblown sons of Gaia.
GREENHORN
Oh, you mean where those brag-gaia-docio giants got their lumps?
TEREUS
Why, the city's phlegra-matic gloss... will actually be its main attraction.
But what god shall be its patron – or patroness?
For whom shall we weave the Sacred Robe?
GREENHORN
Why not let Athena have it?
SILVERTONGUE
What sort of place is this going to be, with a matron as its patron?
A goddess in battledress? Isn't Athena's city already in enough of a mess
with men like Kleisthenes, over there, wearing a woman's dress?
GREENHORN
Who then is going to patrol the city Stockade?
TEREUS
Why, we have just the bird, the one of Persian stock,
so famously fearsome that he's known far-and-wide
– as (ahem) "the war god's cock"!
GREENHORN
Oh, lord the Shag of Persia: Why, that's ideal when you need
a bird to guard the portal rock!
SILVERTONGUE (TO GREENHORN)
Yes, now you've got the idea, and it's time to get things underway:
So off you go! Take off, man, and set-up house with the masons:
it's time to build the walls sky high – but do start with the foundations.
GREENHORN
You mean I should lodge with the masons?
SILVERTONGUE
Yes, but they tend to stonewall: so we need you to fly up there
and oversee all operations...
GREENHORN
But I don't know that much about walls, you know...

SILVERTONGUE
Well, then you'll just have to wing it: strip-yourself-off,
work-yourself-up, come here, go there, climb the ladder,
do the rounds, carry the torch, station the watch,
and if they need something brought, well: you'll have to bring it.
Oh, and fetch-in a couple of heralds: send one up to the gods,
and the other on down to mankind, then get back to me.
GREENHORN
And you, Silvertongue, just stay here behind – and enjoy my misery!
SILVERTONGUE
No: go, do, my good man, er... I'm counting on you:
everything now rests on your shoulders.
(HE TAKES AN UNDERWHELMED LOOK AT GREENHORN'S WINGS)
(Thank god, not on your wings, at least!)
I, however, shall organize a sacrifice to the new gods in town:
hence to summon a presiding priest.

GREENHORN FLIES OFF

Boy! Boy! Fetch the basket of sacrificial barley,
and the tub of lustral water.

THE "HUMAN" SLAVES, NOW FEATHERED, FLY IN WITH THE SACRIFICIAL REQUISITES

CHORUS LEADER
Great minds think alike, that's just the thing,
we agree that's the way to go, so we're ready to sing
a grand processional ode to speed
these most venerable gods along their way.
And in our keep we have a goodwill sheep
to immolate and give 'em.
Come! Come cry a Pythian ode to the god of song
and, god willing, let Chairis actually pipe along
almost in time with the rhythm!

A WELL-KNOWN MUSICIAN FLIES IN, DRESSED AS A CROW, AND PROCEEDS TO PLAY

◇◈◈◈ THE PRIEST ◈◈◈◇

SILVERTONGUE
Stop! Stop your blowing! Herakles, what was that?
By Zeus, I have seen many a downright amazing bird,
but a piper with a bugle like that... I have never heard!

A FEATHERED PRIEST ENTERS, LEADING A VERY LEAN GOAT

Ah, a priest: you're right on cue... a sacrifice to the gods anew,
if you please.
PRIEST
Not a problem: that'd be quite easy to do... er –
if we only had a basket...
(HE LOCATES THE SLAVE WITH THE BASKET, THEN BEGINS LEADING THE PRAYERS:)
All pray to the Kite – the Hestia of the Birds –
their hearthkeeper, and to the Olympian and Olympianess birds,
male and female whomsoever:
– Geetings, O Lord Albatross, Hawk of the Sea...
SILVERTONGUE (INTERJECTING, BUT AS IF RESPONDING IN PRAYER)
– Yes, yea verily: that's good-bye Poseidon, gone forever!
PRIEST (AS BEFORE)
Greetings, O Swan of Pytho and Delos
SILVERTONGUE (AS BEFORE)
– Yea: that's farewell Apollo; good-bye to thee!
PRIEST (AS BEFORE)
O greetings Leto, Mother of Ortuga...
SILVERTONGUE (AS BEFORE)
– Ortuga? Oh, yes: the Island of Quail –
PRIEST (AS BEFORE)
...and to Artemis of the Crow and Sparrow...
SILVERTONGUE (AS BEFORE)
– No more Artemis of the bow and arrow! – All hail...
PRIEST (AS BEFORE)
...and to the Booby Sabazius...

SILVERTONGUE (AS BEFORE)
– Otherwise known as Dionysius: –
PRIEST (AS BEFORE)
and to the great Tit, Mistress Rhea,
mother of gods, and men as well –
SILVERTONGUE
...mother of that great tit Sokrates, the goddamned infidel!
PRIEST (AS BEFORE)
Oh, we beseech ye grant the Cloudcuckoolanders health and security
– oh, and don't forget the allies too... Now let us pray!
SILVERTONGUE (AS BEFORE)
Oh yea! – Yes, don't forget to tack the allies on
as an afterthought in everything you say...
PRIEST (AS BEFORE)
...and to the bird heroes and their offspring,
to the boobie and the nitwit,
and to the turkey and the bigtit,
and to the purple cock and hooker,
and to the peacock and onlooker,
and to the the pillock and the mullard,
and to the dodo and the dullard,
to the dipstick, doofus, dildo...
SILVERTONGUE
Stop! Stop these invocations! Oy vey!
And go to the crows! How big do think this victim is, you curse:
Can't you see that a single raptor could snatch this goat away?
Take your rosaries and hit the road – there's nothing worse,
for it's like they always say: If you want a job done well,
No gain without a little sacrifice – so best to do it yoursel'!

SILVERTONGUE'S SLAVES, PECKING & FLAPPING, CHASE THE PRIEST FROM THE STAGE

CHORUS LEADER
Well then, we'll raise a second song, for you now,

for we can see what needs to be done...
and godfearing, we think we have the solution:
Pious and devout, we'll invoke the blesséd gods again,
but this time we'll call upon just one –
if indeed there's even enough stuff here for even one god to eat –
for this victim, as we can see, is well endowed with horns
and a mean goatee – but precious little meat!
SILVERTONGUE
Yea then, let us pray then
to the wingéd gods, and sacrifice...

POET (ENTERS)
Ahh, Cloudcuckooland – O Muse, confirm it
in thy hymns asinging – is no Fool's Paradise...
SILVERTONGUE
Good God: where's this business come from?
Hey: who the hell're you?
POET
Ah me? – I pour the songs of honey-tongued poetry,
an observant servant of the Muses, according to Homer.
SILVERTONGUE (EYEING THE POET'S REVEALING OUTFIT)
Observant? Well, I'm observant...
that you have too much, er... hair to be a servant!
POET
Well, I'm not a eunuch – yet we artful singers
are all fervent servants of the Muses,
according to Homer.
SILVERTONGUE
Artful? Hmm, and with a tunic... so threadbare
I suppose you have to stay fervent – or you'll freeze.
Nevertheless, O poet, by what undoing are you here?
POET
Why, I have composed, for this – your Cloudcuckooland –

verses both virginal and beautiful, and highfalutin grand
– and deserving of royaltees!

SILVERTONGUE

Royalties, eh? On demand? Hmm, well you sure work fast.
When did you compose these things?

POET

Why I've been singing the praises of your city here
for many ages past.

SILVERTONGUE

But I'm only just now doing the tenth-day dedication,
like with a new-born babe, and the naming celebration...

POET

"But how swift the sayings of the Muses fly,
just like the prancing hooves of horses."

SILVERTONGUE

According to Homer, I suppose?

POET

According to Homer, why...
"thou founding father of the City on the Hill,
thou hast given thy name to things
both divine and full of dread,
Yea, the gift thou granteth by the nod
of thy high and mighty head
– so granteth unto me what unto me thou granteth will."
(HE BOWS & PUTS OUT HIS HAND IN EXPECTATION OF A DONATIVE)

SILVERTONGUE

(ASIDE:) Hmm, this bad smell's going to hang about
unless we can blow him off with some sort of ruse.
(TO ONE OF THE SLAVES)
Hey you: you've got a tunic – and a vest: doff it, quick!
(TO THE POET)
Here, take the vest: it'll help to warm your frigid muse.

POET
Not unwillingly however, does the belovéd Muse
accept this gift: for you, we thank it... now in return
this Pindarian phrase, we bid you learn...
SILVERTONGUE
(ASIDE:) Did I say "bad smell?" Make that "shit to a blanket".
POET
"With the nomads in Scythia
the itinerant sage doth roam:
no woven cloth doth clothe,
yea shameful skin for home
he bears: a vest without a tunic:
a life all men must loathe."
Do gather what I say.
SILVERTONGUE
I gather that you want this eunuch
to doff another layer.
(TO THE SLAVE) Okay, strip for pity's sake.
(TO THE POET) Now take this and go away!
POET
I am going, and in going, to the city,
I give thee another take:
"O Muse on throne of gold,
thou hast answered my every praýer;
thou hast shut out the trembling cold:
I am escaped to the promised land – and shout me hallelujah!"
(EXIT POET)
SILVERTONGUE
(CALLING AFTER HIM) Hallelujah!
That must be the land of the heartwarming snowjob, by Zeus –
and that he caught wind of the city so soon:
I certainly never expected that sort of poetic abuse...
(TO A SLAVE) Okay, take the basin and do the rounds.

(TO ALL) Silence! Let no man hereafter our deeds impugn!
Let there be none but words of happy omen!

ORACLEMONGER (ENTERS, WIELDING A LARGE SCROLL)
Don't start on that goat!
SILVERTONGUE
And who are you?
ORACLEMONGER
Why, I'm obviously a soothsayer... that's who.
SILVERTONGUE
Then bugger off: Can't you see we're about to be...
joining each other in prayer?
ORACLEMONGER
You devil! Make not so light of divine inspiration,
for there is an ancient oracle of the prophet himself –
it's utterly compelling – and spoken specifically for Cloudcuckooland.
SILVERTONGUE
Well, pray why didn't you foretell me about that foretelling
before we founded the fort, er... this new place of dwelling?
ORACLEMONGER
Well, beforehand... I was too tied up in religious prognostication.
SILVERTONGUE (TO THE AUDIENCE)
Well, there's nothing for it but to hear his inevitable obfuscation.
ORACLEMONGER (READING FROM THE SCROLL)
"Lo, when wolves shack up with grizzly crows
somewhere 'twixt Lesbos and the sea..."
SILVERTONGUE
'Twixt the island and the sea? – Hmm, but say:
just what have Lesbians got to do with me?
ORACLEMONGER
Oh, that was just the prophet alluding to the cuckoo.
Hem, "First sacrifice a white-haired goat to Pandora:
and he who comes as the first oracle of my words, you...

shall give to him a clean cloak and new sandals."
SILVERTONGUE
Sandals are in there too?
ORACLEMONGER
Take a look at the book!
"...and to him give a goblet too, and fill his hands with nibblies."
SILVERTONGUE
And "nibblies" is in there too?
ORACLEMONGER
Take a look at the book!
"...and if, however, thou dost that which I enjoin, thou shalt soar
like an eagle in the clouds: but if thou give not, young fellow,
thou shalt be neither woodpecker, nor grapesucker, nor cocksparrow."
SILVERTONGUE
And that's in there as well?
ORACLEMONGER
Take a look at the book!
SILVERTONGUE
But that oracle bears no parallel
to this little riddle – nay, to this little song
from the oracle priestess of Apollo...
(HE PRODUCES A SCROLL, THEN READS:)
– I wrote it out myself, you know –
Ahem: "... if however some quack should come along
uninvited, vexing the sacrifice, and hellbent
on some Hey-diddle-diddle...
then it is fated that he be struck a blow
somewhere in the middle..."
(PRODS THE ORACLEMONGER WITH THE SCROLL)
ORACLEMONGER (RECOVERING HIS BREATH)
I deem that to be a bad reading!
SILVERTONGUE
Take a look at the book!

"...and be sparing of none, not even of the eagle in the sky,
nor of the harrier, nor of the hawker with the evil eye!"
ORACLEMONGER
And that's in there as well?
SILVERTONGUE (THROWING THE BOOK AT THE ORACLEMONGER)
Take a look at the book! (ASIDE:) There, I've thrown the book
at him! (TO THE ORACLEMONGER:) Now go to hell!
ORACLEMONGER (AS HE EXITS, APACE)
Woe! I'm getting the bum's rush from a swooping thrush!
SILVERTONGUE
Surely you're not running-off spruiking-oracles on the side?

METON
(ENTERS, WITH A LARGE RULER & CALIPERS, AND WEARING PLATFORM SHOES)
I have come to you –
SILVERTONGUE
Again! Here's another bugbear...
What are you up to then? Drawing up plans are we?
Well, what's your design? And what's with the tragic footwear?
METON
I need a little leg up, you know... for I am here to subdivide the sky,
so you can sell it off, piecemeal, if you like, er... as apropo'.
SILVERTONGUE
By the gods, sounds like heady stuff: who then, of all men, are you?
METON
Who am I? Why I'm Meton, I'm world famous... why,
I'm well-known all over Greece – and up on the Hill too.
SILVERTONGUE
Well then tell me, Meatonhead, what are these things of yours?
METON
It's Meton, just Meton, and this... is a stave...
a rule, which I shall apply to the sky!
You see, the air as a whole is shaped most like the inside of a cave...

(USING A LARGE URN, LYING ON ITS SIDE, AS A PROP)
I therefore, inserting the stave... run this compass here...
er, over the top - do you get the idea?
SILVERTONGUE
I don't get it.
METON (CHALKING VARIOUS LINES OVER THE URN)
Hem, well: applying the stave at a right angle there
it's easy to see how the circle... becomes a square:
a city square that is – for you – right in the middle:
a meeting and marketplace... with roads radiating,
like with a star, rays emanating from the centre of space...
SILVERTONGUE
The man's a genius! – Meton?
METON
What is it?
SILVERTONGUE
Well, you know... since I'm quite fond of you,
you should let me show... er...
(TAKING THE STAVE AND POINTING TO THE LINES ON THE URN)
you should let me show you the easiest way out,
the easiest way to go... Do you get the idea?
METON (STUDYING THE DIAGRAM)
I don't get it.
SILVERTONGUE (POINTING, AS BEFORE, TO THE LINES ON THE URN)
Well, we're a bit like the Spartans here... you know,
and they... are banishing strangers and driving them out,
and even those... who the lines do toe... or who follow
the straights-and-narrows... well, all around town,
even for them, it often comes to blows!
METON
You're surely not drawing up battle lines, and standing, er...
divided amongst yourselves around here?

SILVERTONGUE
No, by God, certainly not: never fear.
METON
What then?
SILVERTONGUE (BRANDISHING THE STAVE)
Well, it's actually the custom here
– and universally approved –
to peck the eyes and beat the backs
of shysters, fraudsters, humbugs
– and interloping quacks!
(TAPS METON'S BOTTOM WITH THE STAVE)

METON
Oh, now I get it! – er, what's that about the easy way out?
SILVERTONGUE
Oh, I don't think you really get it, because if you got it,
you'd have taken it already... But, I'm happy to let you have it!
Here, let me square your circles for you! (HE STRIKES METON'S BOTTOM)
METON (FLEEING)
Ouch, hey! This is a bum rap! (EXITS RUNNING)
SILVERTONGUE
Well, if you can't beat the rap, the rap'll beat you...
(TOSSES THE RULER AFTER METON) – and that's the rule!

INSPECTOR (ENTERS, IN DRAG, PRODDING HERE & THERE WITH A LONG STICK)
Where's the new satrap?
SILVERTONGUE
Who's this Queen of Spades? And what's that tool?
INSPECTOR
I come as duly chosen inspector,
having been dealt the hand... that includes Cloudcuckooland.
SILVERTONGUE
Card carrying, no doubt? – How'd you turn that trick?

INSPECTOR
Ah, that's the art of the deal, Eagle Scout... a man's gotta be slick:
and a little deal here and there... is usually "good as gold". (WINKS)
Cut me in.
SILVERTONGUE
Well, here, let me show my hand. (PRODUCES METON'S CALIPERS)
There, two of a kind. A lucky pair... So now I'm afraid you'll have to fold.
(POKES THE INSPECTOR'S BELLY)
INSPECTOR (DOUBLING OVER)
Yea by the gods, that's not fair! – Why, I should have stayed in politics:
I was a spin-doctor for Donald Trump, you know.
SILVERTONGUE
For Donald Trump? Well you'll need more than a trump, here,
to turn your tricks: Here, let me show you how to play misere!
(GRABS THE INSPECTOR'S STICK, AND SPINS "HIM" ABOUT WITH IT, LIKE A TOP)
INSPECTOR
What was that for?
SILVERTONGUE
That was just politics... taking a turn for the better.
INSPECTOR
Witnesses! An inspector is being attacked!
SILVERTONGUE
No, that's just the run around. We only take to turncoats,
as a matter of fact. (HE LIFTS THE INSPECTOR'S TUNIC WITH THE STICK.
THERE'S NO SIGN OF A PHALLUS) Aha! And now, let me...
strike a blow – for democracy!
(HE STRIKES THE INSPECTOR'S BOTTOM. "HE" RUNS AND HIDES)
SILVERTONGUE (TO THE AUDIENCE)
Isn't it terrifying, how they're already sending snoops up here,
spying, even before we've had a chance... to consecrate
the city... with a sacrifice to the gods, and then to celebrate
that – with a choral dance?

DECREE-SELLER (ENTERS, READING FROM A SCROLL)
"If a Cloudcuckoolander should perchance wrong an Athenian..."
SILVERTONGUE
What's this again? Another cursèd book? Who are you?
DECREE-SELLER
I am a decree vendor, and I have come here to take a look...
er, no: to sell you some new regulations.
SILVERTONGUE (RECOVERING THE BOOK THROWN AT THE ORACLEMONGER)
Like what?
DECREE-SELLER (READING)
"Cloudcuckoolanders shall make use of just the same measures
and weights and precise calibrations – as do the men of Athens."
SILVERTONGUE (READING)
"And cries-of-pain and other displeasures
shall greet all who make uninvited proclamations
– as do the men of Athens"
DECREE-SELLER
Hey, what do you mean by that? And what're you up to?
SILVERTONGUE (NOW SHARPENING THE STAVE THROWN AT METON)
Well, to be blunt, I'm planning to point-out, to you,
some rather pointed laws! (MENACES THE DECREE-SELLER
WITH HIS IMPROMPTU SPEAR. THE DECREE-SELLER TAKES COVER)
INSPECTOR (RE-APPEARS)
I summon Silvertongue to appear next month on charges of assault.
SILVERTONGUE
You again too? Flushed out, by the looks?
DECREE-SELLER (RE-APPEARS, READING)
"...but anyone found at fault... in driving officials away...
or failing to take them in... according to decree,
to laws laid down in graven stone..."
SILVERTONGUE
Oh, more law books! Oh, bugger me!
INSPECTOR
I'll make you pay... I'll get the upper hand.

I'm gonna write you up a fine of forty-grand!
SILVERTONGUE
Well then, here, let me raise the stakes!
I'll ante up... with a dressing down... (HE TEARS THE INSPECTOR'S SKIRT AWAY)
INSPECTOR
Oh, for heaven's sakes! (FLEES & EXITS)
SILVERTONGUE (TO THE DECREE-SELLER)
And as for you: let's calibrate your measure, shall we?
(PATS THE SACRIFICIAL ALTAR) The measure of the man...
Something about "laying down" and "graven stones"...?
DECREE-SELLER
Stones? Nah, I'm shittin' bricks – so catch me if you can! (FLEES & EXITS)
SILVERTONGUE
Somebody grab her! Hey, won't you stay?
(TO THE SLAVES) Ah well, she's got away...
let's just settle for a goat.
Come on, we'll go inside to cut his throat,
and feed the gods without delay.
(EXEUNT ALL BUT THE CHORUS)

CHORUS
To us now, all mortals shall sacrifice with offerings as they pray,
for we see all, and rule as lords over all, as we survey... the earth.
We protect the flowering buds of fruits... We kill all types of bugs
that come up from the soil... and gnaw upon the roots.
We kill the critters that despoil... fragrant gardens
with outrages both foul and vile... that settle 'pon the trees
and with voracious jaws the budding seeds defile.
However many a creeping and crawling thing the day doth bring,
all meet their end in carnage... wrought beneath our mighty wing!
CHORUS LEADER
On this particular prize-festive day... we seem to hear it proclaimed
at every post: Hem: "Whosoever puts the author of that last tragic play
out of his misery: give that man a penny!"

And "whoever should finally slay those long-dead tyrants of yesterday"
(thus at last to put to bed those tales of Magog planted in one's head
by every two-bit demagogue) – "give that man a pound!"
These proclamations fill the air, you've heard them: they're everywhere...
so in light of these proclamations, we wish here and now to make
a home-grown proclamation of our own:
"If anyone should kill that birdseller Philokrates,
the little Sparrowfartes... give that man a penny";
and give him a pound if he hauls him in alive –
for he strings together finches, and sells 'em at fourpence a bunch of five;
he blows air up thrushes' bums... and displays them at inflated sums;
he stuffs feathers into backbirds' noses – and he does that just for fun!
He keeps live pigeons bound in nets... forced to be stool-pigeons,
no: not pets... but so as to round their buddies up:
yes, they're flesh and feather canards!
Those are the proclamations we wished to make:
and if anyone of you is keeping birds imprisoned in your yards...
we advise you to release them straightaway –
for if you're not persuaded to obey... you'll be rounded-up by the chorús,
and tit-for-tat, be forced to act... as sitting-ducks for us!
CHORUS
Blesséd the race of birds on-the-wing, who need wrap no cloak
in winter to keep us dry: for we winter with the mountain nymphs,
where we frolic through dale and dell... and shelter in hollow alcoves,
and skit about pell mell... Nor are we stifled by the summer sun:
her radiant beams we ne'er decry... but in blossoming groves we dwell,
and in lush meadows we wallow and have fun!
Yes, summertime: while all around we hear that sound,
the melody shrill of the cicada – the uncanny, the divine voice –
mad-for-the-sun they are, and in the heat of those long hot days,
basking, they rejoice. – And springtime? Well, in springtime...
we dwell in the Graces garden, and there we graze
the virgin white-mealed myrtle-berries, and sing our songs of praise.
(EXEUNT)

CHORUS LEADER

Now for a word to the judges about the festival prize, how,
if they should judge us best, we will reward them all-and-one;
and how much better the gifts they'll get than those got by Priam's son!
That's Paris, of course: for, as you'll recall, when called upon, he chose –
poor boy – of all the goddesses, Aphrodite as far the most beautiful one.
And what did he get for his trouble... but the love of Helen of Troy!
Yes, yes: the most beautiful woman in Greece, and some say:
to Aphodite a body double... But you! You'll get what every judge
is most willing... to take into account: namely, those owls
minted on every Athenian shilling! They'll flock to you
like homing pigeons, and actually make themselves at home
in your gables and your kegs... and they'll nest in your purses,
and hatch little coinages, like geese laying great golden eggs!
And moreover your houses will be mansions as grand as great temples,
for we'll provide flying butresses to add extra wings;
and if you've got public office... and get accused of being a crook...
just because you've pilfered a few things...
we know a talonted legal eagle, a real hawk,
who'll insert some claws in the laws – to get you off the hook!
And if you're dining-out somewhere,
and someone else's paid for the goat:
we'll show you the trick of tucking that little bit extra...
into the crop of the throat... But! – if you don't decide for us,
then find yourselves great canopies to wear, like every statue does,
to prevent us birds from shitting on its head...
For if the Birds fails to win First Prize,
and you're out-and-about in a nice clean cloak...
perhaps innocently buying a loaf of bread...
that's precisely when justice shall be granted us,
for that's precisely when every bird – no joke!
– will just happen to be having a crap... while flapping overhead!

SILVERTONGUE (ENTERS, REMOVING A BLOODY APRON)
The auspices, O birds, are good for us:
but no messenger has come yet, with tidings from the wall...
and Greenhorn was supposed to get back to me...
(A MESSENGER SHOUTS, WITHIN) *But lo, I hear a call...*
and here comes someone running, like that river god,
Meander, who lost his way... on his way to the sea.
FIRST MESSENGER (ENTERS, RUNNING LEFT & RIGHT, AND OUT OF BREATH)
Whe... where's, whe... where's Sil-, whe... where's Silver-,
oh, whe... where's our fearless leader?
SILVERTONGUE
Here!
FIRST MESSENGER (GASPING)
Oh! Your wall is all built.
SILVERTONGUE
Well said!
FIRST MESSENGER (WITH RECOVERED BREATH)
Oh yes, it's a magnificent piece of work,
a marvel of pompous exaggeration, and so wide on top
that both Elon Musk and Donald Trump, or some other boastful jerk –
chariots opposed, and with their usual trojan horses under yoke –
could surpass each other again and again on those lofty heights...
in a duel for bragging rights.
SILVERTONGUE
No joke? Hercules, what a labour!
FIRST MESSENGER
Yes, without a word of a lie, this tale is genuinely tall...
I measured it myself, and from top to tail, as the crow doth fly...
it's a one-hundred-fathom fall!
SILVERTONGUE
Oh Poseidon, what a wall! – But how was it done?
Who did the work?
FIRST MESSENGER
Just us birds, no-humans at all: not a one!

No Egyptians carrying bricks, no Athenian masons cutting stone,
no Greek tradesman turning tricks: we did it on our own!
From out of Lybia came about thirty-thousand pelicans,
spitting out stones from their beaks, you know, not their bellicans;
and another ten-thousand storks carried bricks,
which the chiselbeaks then honed with their, er... peckers...
and from below into the air, cranes and curlews fetched up water...

SILVERTONGUE

My word! But how did they carry up mud and mortar?

FIRST MESSENGER

Mudlarks, of course... each skylarking with a hod.

SILVERTONGUE

But how did they manage to get the mortar in, by god?

FIRST MESSENGER

The geese, strutting, flipped it in like shovels with their feet.
It was a most ingenious innovation: uplifting, constructive...

SILVERTONGUE

At last: the goosestep has achieved a feat...
that's neither warlike nor destructive!

FIRST MESSENGER

And, by Zeus, there were plenty of chicks there, wearing suspenders
to help them carry bricks there... And they laid them on their backs,
so naturally, when that happened, up went every stork in sight,
tools poised – to poke their putty in the cracks!

SILVERTONGUE

Well, at that rate, why would anybody hire a contractor?
Now, let's see, what else? Er, who finished off the woodworks?

FIRST MESSENGER

Why, the woodpeckers, and the master toma-hawks,
'twas they hatch... hatched... hacheted out the gates and hatches...

SILVERTONGUE

Gesundheit!

FIRST MESSENGER

Ta! ... And now everything there is battened-down with gates,

and bolted-up with latches... There are watch-towers all-around,
and guards and beakoners perched in every tower;
the rounds are made, and the sentinel's bell: it sounds on every hour.
But I'll be running-off, I'm a bit peckish: so the rest is up to you.
(EXITS)

CHORUS LEADER
Hey you, what's the matter? Are you finding it hard to believe
that a bunch of birds were so fast to build a wall?
SILVERTONGUE
Yes, by the gods, I am, and rightly so: for as far as I can tell,
he was telling the truth when he said his tale... was genuinely tall!
But, why, here's another messenger coming this way,
and he's running like a bustard... Why, it's a guard from the wall,
and he's certainly in a flap; why, he's looking positively flustered!
SECOND MESSENGER (ENTERS, ARMED, ALMOST DANCING IN AGITATION)
Ahoy hoy! Ahoy hoy! Ahoy hoy!
SILVERTONGUE
What's going on here?
SECOND MESSENGER
A most terrible thing... has been visited upon us!
One of the gods – one of Zeuses lot – has just now flown
with flapping wing... in mid-air through the gates!
SILVERTONGUE
What about the guards?
SECOND MESSENGER
Well, the nightowls were on day watch: they didn't see a thing!
SILVERTONGUE
O what a dirty trick, a deliberate provocation!
Which of the gods?
SECOND MESSENGER
We don't know: but he has wings, if that's any indication?
SILVERTONGUE
Well, what about the flying squads... the birds with claws?

Were they sent out to intercept? The birds of prey, the raptōrs?
SECOND MESSENGER
Oh, yes, of course... We scrambled three squadrons
of mounted archer-storks... and all those with crooklike talon:
the kestrel, falcon, owl and eagle, and the triple-cocked policy hawks.
They've all spread-out, and in search of the god they swarm –
why, the air's awhir with the force of their wings,
and they're whipping-up a storm...

A VIOLENT GUST SWEEPS THE STAGE

Good god! Lookout there! Why, that's no bird!
That's him, the god: he's on the approach already!
SILVERTONGUE
Then we've no choice but to take up... er, slings!
And bows! Call out the reserves!

SLAVES AND CHORUS RUSH IN, ALL ARMED

Arch your bows! Fire Arrows! And hey: somebody fling me a sling!
CHORUS
So it's war, unspeakable war, a war of nerves,
and not just some unspoken war of words,
broken out now between the gods and us birds!
But guard all now the cloud-girt sky, which Darkness bore,
that someone of the gods not go passing us by
without our notice, like he did before.
(THE CHORUS FORMS A PHALANX AROUND SILVERTONGUE)
CHORUS LEADER
Quiet! Silence! Peel your eyes and look all around,
open your ears and you'll hear the sound,
of an airborne divinity's whirling wings.
Why, that's him: he's here upon us!

IRIS, WITH HUGE IRIDESCENT WINGS, ENTERS, HOVERING LEFT & RIGHT IN THE AIR

SILVERTONGUE
Hey, you, girlie! halt that runaround!

Who art thou? And whence hast thou come?
(CHASING HER LEFT & RIGHT) And to where, to where,
to where are you flying?

IRIS DESCENDS, AS IF TO LAND

That's it: keep calm: stay just there. (HE LUNGES AT HER)
IRIS (FLITS UP OUT OF REACH)
From the gods, I am: one of the Olympians!
SILVERTONGUE
Oh yeah? Summer or Winter: which? (HE LUNGES AGAIN)
IRIS (FLITTING LEFT & RIGHT, IN THE AIR, AS SHE IS CHASED)
What? I am Iris! The rainbow. Messenger of the gods. An angel!

THE CHORUS GASPS WITH EVERY REPEAT OF THE VIEW UP HER SKIRTS

SILVERTONGUE
Uh-huh, of Death or Taxes? (HE LUNGES AGAIN)
IRIS (FLITS AGAIN)
Taxes?
SILVERTONGUE
Taxes! Can't one of you horny policy hawks collect this fiscal, er...
this fickle, er... this flighty bitch?
IRIS
Collect me? What evil's this then? I have every right to expect,
by Zeus, that you'd down on your kness and respect me!
SILVERTONGUE
Fat chance, you mole... now say:
by which gate did you make your way?
How did you penetrate the wall?
IRIS
By which gate, by Zeus? I have no idea at all.
SILVERTONGUE
Do you hear how she dissembles? She's playing loose!
Well, did you screw the head-jay, you brazen slut?
Did the storks punch your ticket while you were underway?

IRIS
What the hell are you talking about? What's all this smut?
SILVERTONGUE
So no cock either made a pass at you nor gave you one?
IRIS
None, by Zeus! I heard no hard word from any bird!
SILVERTONGUE
And so you just sail on through without a peep, and into airspace
that's a bird's by right – and by age-old inheritance… is their space!
IRIS
But where else is it meet for us gods to make our flights?
SILVERTONGUE
I certainly don't know, by Zeus: but certainly not anywhere here.
You're breaking the law even now, you know. In fact, by rights,
you of any rainbow… would desrve to find your end is near!
IRIS
But I'm immortal!
SILVERTONGUE
Yes, and this'd be the end of you all the same, with any luck,
for if we rule everything else, but you Olympians run amok,
what sort of world will it be for us?
You've got to bow to the fact that we're now the top act,
and there's now a pecking order – and we're on top!
Now tell me: where are you headed?
IRIS
Me? I am making tracks – no time to stop –
from the Father of Heaven to those humans way down there…
It's my job to show… that offerings are due – of roast lamb,
and beef barbeque – whose heavenly smells fill the ways of the air
whenever I paint a rainbow!
SILVERTONGUE
Say what? To which gods, say you?
IRIS
To which? To us, of course; to the gods in heaven, to be precise.

SILVERTONGUE
So you are the gods?
IRIS
Well, who else is a god?
SILVERTONGUE
Well, birds are gods to humans now, and to us, by god,
they must sacrifice – and not, by Zeus, to Zeus!
IRIS (FINALLY NOTICING THOSE BELOW GAWKING UP HER SKIRTS)
You unthinking fools! Don't idly inflame
the gods' frightening spleen most dire...
lest thou hasten thy race to destruction – under balls of fire!
Justice Divine hurling thunderbolts like that arsonist of tragic fame,
your-selves and -cities overturning; you with enfolding flame aburning!
SILVERTONGUE
Listen love: stop with the boilerplate Euripidean...
hold your fire, hold steady! I see, come: which is it:
a Lybian or some Trans-Aegean
you think with this fancy talk to be frightening?
And know this, I say: if Zeus vex me further,
the rooftops of his Earthly dwellings
I shall blitz like lightning... with fire-bearing eagles Sophoklean!
And sprays of petrels upon him shall be lit, gigantic plumes
shall fill the heavens as birds of prey destroy the rooms
of his ivory towers and his marbled mansions...
pecking away at their Ionic looms... and their Doric stanchions!
– You though, if you vex me one bit more, the rainbow,
Iris, shall be spreadeagled – one leg east and the other leg west –
and coming at it from below, I shall strike the pot-of-gold
at the central plumbing... and all the world will wonder
how such an old man... can get it up for a second-coming!
IRIS
Ha, such talk is hardly desirous – and I seriously doubt that you can!
SILVERTONGUE
Beat it, Big Tit! Beat those wings! Set sail! Aren't you "fleeting", Iris!

IRIS
Sure as eggs my father will lay you out for such a fowl tongue!
(SHE DELIBERATELY FLARES HER SKIRTS TO TEASE ALL BELOW AS SHE DEPARTS)

SILVERTONGUE
Oh wretched me! Surely flirting, er... flitting elsewhere then
you could be burning-up someone young!
CHORUS
We have shut-out the gods of Zeus begot
They'll no-longer pass through our city,
nor yet any devotional from a sacrificial floor
can get through as smoke to the gods anymore.
SILVERTONGUE
It's a bit of a worry that the herald we sent
to the mortals has disappeared –
CHORUS LEADER
...and if he never comes back the way he went
it would be exceedingly weird!

HERALD (ENTERS BEARING A GOLDEN WREATH)
O Silvertongue, O Blesséd One, O Most-wise,
O Most-famous, O Most-wise, O Most-slick,
O Thrice-blessed, O tell me when to stop!
SILVERTONGUE
Okay, get on with it: What's your shtick?
HERALD (PLACING THE WREATH ON SILVERTONGUE'S HEAD)
O Silvertongue, on account of your wisdom
and your earthly renown,
and on behalf of all of the people,
with this wreath, I thee crown.
SILVERTONGUE
I accept. But why do the people honour me thus?
HERALD
Why? Because you're the founder of this most glorious aetherial town!

You do not know how great the esteem you bear among men –
oh, what a fuss! – and how many the lovers of this place: no small few!
Before this particular city was founded by you, you'd...
why, everyone was mad about Sparta way back then:
they grew their hair long, made like Sokrates, and went without food;
they never washed neither, and they sported leatherbound sticks
– not as real cipher-rods... but as false Spartan pricks!
But now, they've gone about-face, and worshipping birds as their gods,
you can see them all over the place... they've caught the bird craze,
everyone having a great time, no limitations, acting like birds,
doing perfect bird imitations. – They start their days
at the very crack of dawn, all at once flying straight out of bed
and – like we do – down to the law...

CHORUS LEADER (ASIDE)
...to the lawn...

HERALD
...then, before long they're into the weeds, and looking to issue
equitable provisions they peck through the leaves...

CHORUS LEADER (ASIDE)
...of their law books...

HERALD
...checking each of the branches...

CHORUS LEADER (ASIDE)
...of law...

HERALD
...for equitable deeds.

CHORUS LEADER (ASIDE)
...for edible seeds.

HERALD
They have birdmania so bad that it's a downright pandemic,
and bird names have even been given to many a well-known man:
why, there's Robin Williams, Walter Pidgeon, Russell Crowe,
and a Nightingale named Florence... there's a Quail called Dan,
a Wren called Christopher, and a very tall Bird called Lawrence...

SILVERTONGUE
Huh?
CHORUS LEADER
Larry Bird.
SILVERTONGUE
Oh!
HERALD
....and there's Steven Seagull, and the cockfighting crew,
whose roundhouse kicks a man is no chicken to duck
– let me tell you – if he wants to avoid a broken skull!
In fact, everyone's quite chirpy, for love of chicks,
full of pluck, singing songs with catchy lyrïcs
where something about birds can be heard in the words,
be it some bit about boobies, or some love for a dove, or a tit,
or a shag, or even just a bit of feather or fluff!
Well, that's it: that how things with men sit,
but let me just tell you one other thing more:
those humans, they just can't get enough –
so thousands of them are on their way here, to your door,
and they're wanting wings, and makeovers to talons,
and other transformative stuff!
SILVERTONGUE
Well, by Zeus, we've no business just standing around!
We'll have to find 'em feathers and wings and other bird things...
(TO A SLAVE AS THE HERALD DEPARTS)
Say you, quick, get some baskets and wings and make up some hampers,
and get Jeeves to fetch 'em out here to me. I however
shall receive these new converts: we want none but happy-campers!
(THE SLAVE GOES IN)

CHORUS LEADER
There'll soon be more cocks in this city
than there ever was in an old Corinthian whore... er, henhouse.

CHORUS
Yet Fortune is a fickle mistress, and there's an air
of uncanny expectation. What will happen? Who can say?
Still, the passion for this city of ours will rule the day...

JEEVES ENTERS, BRINGING A BASKETFULL OF WINGS, ETC.

SILVERTONGUE (TO JEEVES)
I say, Jeeves: can't you fetch 'em in faster than that then?

JEEVES HURRIES OFFSTAGE

CHORUS
...for what's not in her that's not good for men
looking to sow wild oats in a greener pasture?
She has Wisdom, Desire, immortal Grace,
and of benevolent Tranquility, the beautiful face.

JEEVES HAS RE-ENTERED WITH ANOTHER BASKETFULL OF TRAPPINGS, BUT DALLIES TO ENJOY THE PROMISED TRANQUILITY

SILVERTONGUE
By Jeeves, what slovenly service! Can't you idle a little faster?
Go on: get someone to fetch a crate of wings, and you –
don't forget who's slave and who's master!
(HE BEATS HIS WINGS AT JEEVES, WHO COWERS AND RETREATS)
CHORUS LEADER
Why's this one so slow?
SILVERTONGUE
Oh, that's Jeeves: he's a dodo, you know.
CHORUS LEADER
Oh, but have you got the hang of giving orders by pecking?
(THREATENS TO PECK JEEVES, WHO HURRIES OFFSTAGE)
You see: things have to be made painfully clear,
and even we birds have to maintain social order:
the musical wings here... the prophetic ones there,
and them with all the flashy maritime gear...

JEEVES RE·ENTERS, AND STARTS TO HELP HIMSELF TO A FITTING OF WINGS

...and of course, when fitting a man out with wings,
you need to size him up with discretion and care...
SILVERTONGUE
Good Hawkins, Jeeves, didn't you get the pecking order?
Well, take it from me...
(CHASES JEEVES LEFT & RIGHT, PECKING AT HIM UNTIL HE RUNS OFFSTAGE)

PARRICIDE (ENTERS, SINGING:)
"Oh, I wish I were an eagle soaring high over the swelling sea..."
SILVERTONGUE
Hmm, it seems that herald wasn't just whistling dick-see!
Here's someone inspired to sing in praise of the eagle...
PARRICIDE
Wa-hoo! there's nothing sweeter than to be on the wing...
SILVERTONGUE
Ahoy there, young man, what are you up to?
I hope you're not another shyster just here to inveagle...
PARRICIDE:
Me? No! Not at all! No, I am bird-crazy,
and I'm here with a question, er... paralegal –
for I want to live as free as a bird,
so I want to partake of your customs and laws.
SILVERTONGUE
Hmm, which laws? For birds have many customs, you know,
that are not codified in any ironclad clause...
PARRICIDE
Why, I like them all, but the one I'd most rather...
is the one where it's customary among birds to throttle
and peck at the neck of one's father!
SILVERTONGUE
Well, by Zeus, we do deem it jolly good form to choke the old cock,
even if you're too young to go at it alone, er... Yes, that's not bad.

PARRICIDE
Indeed, that's why I want to become part of your flock,
for I have my heart set on putting the squeeze on my dad,
and on getting my claws... into all that he has.
SILVERTONGUE
Ah, not so fast... for it happens that there's just been passed... er,
new legislation: a couple of laws... er, to do with nest-egg reuse
and er, let's see... ah yes: seasonal migration...
(HE HAS SNATCHED UP A SCROLL AND NOW PRETENDS TO READ)
stating whereas, er... that "after the father has done his best
vis-à-vis er... conception and incubation...
er... the fully-fledged youth must return to the nest...
and make some contribution... to the old cock's superannuation!"
PARRICIDE
What! But what return do I get, by Zeus,
having come here with visions of revolution...
if indeed it's for me to feed... that hoary old bustard now!
SILVERTONGUE
Oh, no, no, not at all! Since you came here, my boy, in such good will
– as if you were an orphan chick – I shall fledge you anyhow!
Now let me admonish you to no evil, my young man,
but to that which I learned myself when I was a lad:
Never shit in your own nest, and never strike at your dad!
Now, take this here wing, and with your cockspur well in hand,
visualize yourself with a mighty crest...

PARRICIDE, WITH PHALLUS IN ONE HAND, HOLDS THE WING
ATOP HIS HEAD, LIKE A CREST, WITH THE OTHER

...that's the way! Now Ten-hut! About face! Forward march!
Left, Right, Left, Right... that's the way!
Now, you can support yourself – on army pay!
Yes, let your father live; but afterwards if you're still spoiling
for some action, then fly off to that there Thracian front,
and finding yourself a made man, get your fill of ...

PARRICIDE
Oh, yes! A Thracian maid! Wa-hoo! I'm inspired,
by Dionysos – and by you – and I'm on the wing again!
(MARCHES OFF, PHALLUS IN HAND, STILL HOLDING THE WING UP LIKE A CREST)
SILVERTONGUE
What good sense you're showing, by Zeus.

KINESIAS (ENTERS, SINGING & DANCING. HE IS VERY LANKY)
"Lo, lo, la-la... to Olympus on lissom wings I fly:
aflutter on the melodic line – flippng here, flopping yon..."
SILVERTONGUE
O woebegone! – this one's going to take a whole bagfull of wings!
KINESIAS (SINGING & DANCING)
"...yet an unflappable soul... that's me... I come and go..."
SILVERTONGUE
There's only one man in Greece who that could be...
Greetings, Kinesias, human beanpole!
What brings you here afoot, turning circles with thy pigeon toe?
KINESIAS
Why, I wish to become a warbling songbird, with a voice to echo
er... through the land.
SILVERTONGUE
Then stop wobbling on those lanky legs, and trying to sound so grand!
Come, explain yourself, for it's true... you know: that stuff you sing:
it's hard on the ear, but it's even harder to understand!
KINESIAS
Well, I've come to get wings from you... so that, flying high,
I can catch highfalutin, er... newfangled snatches of air-tossed
and snowclad compositions... from out the cloudy sky.
SILVERTONGUE
Is that actually possible?
KINESIAS
Possible? Why, without it, this art of ours would be wholly incognoscible!
For the shining-bits of dithyrambs, you see,

are born caliginous and crepuscular, yet airy and obscure:
lend me your ears, and I'll give you a grandiose tour!

SILVERTONGUE

Oh, no you won't!

KINESIAS

Oh yes, by Poseidon, I will.
Here, let me run through the whole air for you:
(HE SINGS:)
"With visions of wildly whirling oarlike wings,
of aero-nautical, acro-batical, er...
of gangly, gobbling, goose-necked raptors,
running like the wind..."

SILVERTONGUE

(GOES OVER TO THE CRANK OF A LARGE CIRCULAR FAN, WHOSE BLADES ARE FEATHERED, LIKE WINGS)

Ahoy there, matey! That's weigh 'nough, already!
Check it down! Luff up! Avast!"

KINESIAS (SINGING & DANCING)

"Oh, to run a course athwart the currents,
driven by each blustering blast..."

SILVERTONGUE

Time to wind it up, by Thunder!
(HE STARTS TO CRANK THE FAN, WHICH – WITH HAMMERS ON ITS SPOKES STRIKING SPECIALLY-TUNED BARS – TAPS OUT THE CYCLIC TUNE OF A WELL-KNOWN SHANTY)
Yea, I shall put an end to these blustering blasts of yours!

KINESIAS (SINGING, FACING THE FAN)

"Fa-fa-facing-up to life's adverse winds, I refuse to hunker under...

SILVERTONGUE PULLS THE RIPCORD ON A BAG SUSPENDED ABOVE THE FAN, DIRECTING A STREAM OF FEATHERS AT KINESIAS, WHO TURNS HIS BACK ON THEM

...for the intrepid sailor turns his back
on both the critic and the fan,
and leaves his mark like a wake in the air,
a remarkable mark of a man!"

◇◈◈◈ THE INFORMER ◈◈◈◇

THE STREAM OF FEATHERS HAS ABATED, BUT THOSE THAT STRUCK
KINESIAS HAVE STUCK TO HIM. SILVERTONGUE STOPS CRANKING,
AND THE MELODY OF THE MUSICAL WINDMILL SLOWS TO A CLUNKY FINALEAnd I
thought all the most devious devices were in my compositions!

SILVERTONGUE
Well, I thought you came here hoping to become fully-fledged?
KINESIAS
Ha, this is a fine way to treat the teacher of the cyclic chorus,
to whom direction of the tragic chorus has been pledged...
and over which, of course, the ten tribes of Athens are always in...
er... dramatic competitions!
SILVERTONGUE
Well, you're welcome to stay here, and your stuff to teach –
although we find it quirky... Why, you could even teach
a chorus of gangly gobbling goose-necked raptors
to each of the ten ancient tribes – of Turkey!
KINESIAS (HAUGHTILY)
Well, you can take the piss... but to me a tragic chorus
is just no laughing matter... so know this:
I am certainly not going to change my ways,
to leave my tragic art behind, nor to grow a feather fatter!
(EXITS IN A CONCEITED HUFF, AS AN INFORMER ENTERS, TAKING NOTES ON A TABLET)

INFORMER (TO HIMSELF)
A few tits... a couple of boobies... a swallow, and a cock...
SILVERTONGUE
Good grief, what this? Looks like something the cat's dragged in...
INFORMER (TO SILVERTONGUE)
What's up, Old Cock? What's up?
SILVERTONGUE
...and as wet as a shag on a rock...
INFORMER (CRUDELY)
What? A wet pussy too, Old Cock?

SILVERTONGUE (SOMEWHAT REPELLED)
Is that "Old Cock" or "old cloak"?
INFORMER (OVERLY FAMILIAR)
Say: Is that another "worn out" joke? Another old ragtime tune...?
SILVERTONGUE (COOLLY)
Why? Have you come hoping to sing for your dinner?
INFORMER
No, say, you look like an upstanding bloke... Where...
(LOOKS AROUND, AS IF TO CHECK THAT NOBADY CAN OVERHEAR)
...can I get a nice big pair?
SILVERTONGUE (LOOKS AROUND, SIMILARLY)
Of wings?
INFORMER
Of wings.
SILVERTONGUE
Well, you've come to just the right place,
but what's with all this cloak, er... and dagger?
INFORMER (LOOKING AROUND)
Shhh! I'm under cover... just in case...
SILVERTONGUE (IN A LOUD WHISPER)
In case of what? You're not going to turn-coat, I hope?
INFORMER
Nope, by Zeus, just the opposite. Here: let me give you the dope:
I – am a spy: I keep an eye on any ally... who steps out of line:
These islanders, you know...
SILVERTONGUE
Oh, so you're an informer... What a happy trade!
INFORMER
And litigator too... If an islander does even the slightest thing wrong,
I sue... Accordingly, it would make life a lot easier if I could, er...
get a bird's eye view... then swoop – and bang! – serve a summons.
SILVERTONGUE
But won't feathers tend to get stuck in your throat?
It'll be pretty hard to summon anyone when you're hoarse.

INFORMER
God no, no ifs, ands, buts, or maybies:
wings will let me fly free of pirates: I won't have to go by boat...
and then, of course... I can dig up dirt like a shovelbill crane,
and deliver summons like a stork does babies!
SILVERTONGUE
So you, a young man, want to make a living
by digging-up dirt on strangers, and playing midwife to their woes?
INFORMER
"What's the harm?" as the saying goes,
besides: I don't know how to work a farm.
SILVERTONGUE
But, by Zeus, there are other more respectable jobs
by which a man could make ends meet.
You know, from legitimate things,
like in all the generations that have gone before...
rather than this patchwork cloak of pettifogging deceit
– and wholecloth fabrications of suits at law.
INFORMER
O Mister, fledge me, don't sledge me.
SILVERTONGUE
I am: by wording-you-up I give you wings... with every word I speak.
INFORMER
And how by wordiness do you give a man wings?
SILVERTONGUE
What a question from a geek! Why, everything
to do with words sets the wings aflapping...
INFORMER
Everything?
SILVERTONGUE
Haven't you heard how fathers in barbershops talk about you
young men, saying "Oh, that boy of mine, how shocked I am:
just hearing word of a new horse going through its paces,
why, "he's up and flown-off," he'll say "...to the races!"

Then another will say of his own that, having turned to writing
tragedy, he's been set in a flutter, and his mind sent all aflap...
INFORMER
Well, it is a load of ...
SILVERTONGUE
I'll say. For by words the mind is both put up in the air,
and a man roused-up to act like a jerk...
it can work its magic either way.
Thus even you – by apropriate words –
I am hoping to set on the wing,
thus to get you fully-fledged...
by a turn to traditional work.
INFORMER
Well then save your breath: I'm already pledged.
SILVERTONGUE
Why? What do you mean?
INFORMER
Well, I can't take up another trade, that'd let my family down.
I come from a long long line of informers, don't you see:
it's in my blood, it's my inheritance, and my family's ancestral work.
It's been handed down from generation to generation,
and now it's been left up to me... and to tell the truth,
it's a responsibility I refuse to shirk... So just fledge me
with the fleet and nimble wings of a kestrel, let's say –
or a hawk– so that while the islanders are still under way,
under sail hither to answer the summons – well, then,
I can beat them with the wings of a swift and speedy trial,
and then beat them back home again!
SILVERTONGUE
Oh, I see... hither and tither: a double beating...
INFORMER
Yes. Hither and tither.
SILVERTONGUE
With some poor foreigner getting an adverse judgement here, while...

INFORMER
...while he's still underway! In absentia, don't you see?
And then...
SILVERTONGUE
Oh, I see! And then... While he's limping home,
you'll have already flown back over there again...
INFORMER
...to seize his propertÿ!
SILVERTONGUE
It'll be fait accompli!
INFORMER
Precisély! – I'll just whip across from A to B...
It requires nothing but wings... and a beeline by me!
SILVERTONGUE
A beeline? Oh yes, I see... you'll whip across... a double beating...
INFORMER
Oh, yes, I'll be as busy as a bee...
SILVERTONGUE
A worker bee!
INFORMER
A worker bee!
SILVERTONGUE
Well then, let me see... (RUMMAGES THROUGH A BASKET)
...by Zeus, I have just the things (PRODUCING A DOUBLE-THONGED WHIP)
to help you whip across the sea... Korkurian wings!
INFORMER
Oh bugger me... I want wings not a whip.
SILVERTONGUE
No, not a whip: a whipping, actuallÿ... for with these... today,
I am going to help you earn your stripes, like all the other bees!
(STARTS CRACKING THE WHIP AT THE INFORMER'S FEET)
INFORMER (LEAPING)
Yipes! Oh gees!

SILVERTONGUE
That's the way!

THE INFORMER TRIES TO SNATCH A PAIR OF WINGS AS HE DODGES THE WHIP

Now, don't delay! It's time you learned to Take off!
(CRACKS THE WHIP AGAIN)
There's a bittersweet serve of poetic justice
just waiting for you in the wings.

THE INFORMER RUNS OFF-STAGE

Come on boys, let's grab these things.
He'll soon discover that the sleazebug shyster is a game two can play
– and that the honey bee stings.

EXEUNT, TAKING BASKETS, ETC.

CHORUS
There's many a newfangled and amazing and terrible thing
we have overflown... Why, there is begot a strange and flighty tree,
whose heart is more hollow than Kleonymoos' is shaky –
it's good for nothing, really just yellow and overblown... In spring
it always squibs, and loves to drop big fibs... er figs, you see –
but come the storm it yields its leafy shield, for just like him, it's flaky!
CHORUS LEADER
There is moreover a place beyond, all dark, no light,
and even of candlelight bereft,
where heroes and men dwell and dine together all day,
but none dare go out at night...
For if anyone happens upon our snowdropping Orestes,
he'll be sure to be struck with fright,
and – stripped of his cloak – frozen, he'll be left,
with no mortal witness to swear on his testes...
to help him uphold his right!

PROMETHEUS (ENTERS, DRESSED AS A BRIDE, VEILED, AND CARRYING A PARASOL)
Oh, speaking of bereft... Ye gods, don't let Zeus find me!
– and where is Silvertongue?
SILVERTONGUE (ENTERS, CARRYING A POTTY)
Oho, what's this? A wedding? That's the first I've heard of it.
PROMETHEUS
Hey, psst! Do you see any of the gods up there, behind me?
SILVERTONGUE
By Zeus, I certainly don't, young, er... and who are you?
PROMETHEUS
No, first tell me, pray: What is the time of day?
SILVERTONGUE
The time of day? Why, are you late for something?
And who are you, anyhow?
PROMETHEUS
Would an old god be ready for an afternoon nap about now?
What do you think?
SILVERTONGUE
Well, you're putting me to sleep.
PROMETHEUS
But tell me, can you say what Zeus's up to?
Gathering the clouds? – or clearing them away?
SILVERTONGUE
Well, I think Zeus is feeling, er... blue, but I predict grey skies for you!
PROMETHEUS
In that case, I think it's safe to unveil.
(FLICKS THE VEIL BACK OVER HIS HEAD)
SILVERTONGUE
O Prometheus, old friend!
PROMETHEUS
Stop! Stop! Keep it down!
SILVERTONGUE
What is it?

PROMETHEUS
Be quiet, and don't call me by name, for starters:
I'm lying low – from Zeus: if he sees me here, he'll cook my, er...
(LOOKS ABOUT CAUTIOUSLY) *he'll have my guts for garters...*
But I'm here to tell you all about what's going on up there...
so take this parasol and keep me covered,
so the gods can't see me from the air.

SILVERTONGUE
Oho, what genius! What foresight! Why, you really are Prome...

PROMETHEUS
Shhh!

SILVERTONGUE
...thian. ...thian. Promethian. Er, now, get under here quick,
and then you can spill your, er... you can have your say.

PROMETHEUS
Okay... now listen carefully.
(THERE'S A LONG PAUSE AS HE CAUTIOUSLY LOOKS LEFT & RIGHT)

SILVERTONGUE
I'm all ears.

PROMETHEUS (AFTER ANOTHER CAUTIOUS PAUSE)
Zeus... has had his day... He's washed up. Finished. Done for.
(THERE'S ANOTHER LONG PAUSE AS SILVERTONGUE WAITS FOR MORE INFORMATION)

SILVERTONGUE
Finished, you say? Since when?

PROMETHEUS (LOOKING LEFT & RIGHT AGAIN, BEFORE HE SPEAKS)
Why, from the day you colonized the air.
Not a single human sacrifices to the gods anymore... not one,
and without the savoury aroma of thigh-bones wafting up
like it did before... it's like being a new bride and going without,
(RUBS HIS CROTCH) *er... at the Thesmophoria!*
On the other hand, the barbarian gods are so hungry,
they're bellyaching like Babylonians, and Zeus is being extorted...
They're threatening to march down on him
if he doesn't bring about a re-opening of the markets –

especially the meat-markets – so that their cut
of tasty inner thigh can be once again imported!
SILVERTONGUE
So there are other gods, foreign ones, upcountry from you?
PROMETHEUS
How could there not be outlandish gods up there?
Who'd fill the family tree of interlopers like Jonah, the...?
SILVERTONGUE
Oh yes, the Wandering Jew... But these barbarian gods:
What are they called? Do they have a tribal affiliation?
PROMETHEUS
Tribal? I'll say, in fact they're called the Tribulati:
a most uncouth and intemperate goddamned nation.
SILVERTONGUE
Oh, that must be where that word comes from.
PROMETHEUS
What word? Tribal?
SILVERTONGUE
No, tribulation.
PROMETHEUS
Most likely. But I can tell you one thing for sure:
ambassadors will be coming here – from Zeus –
seeking some sort of peaceful reconciliation... and from
these trumpian Tribulati, keen on skipping ahead to the libation...
But if there's no transfer of Zeuses sceptre back to the birds,
and if you don't get Sovereigntina given to you, to take as wife,
then don't even think about putting a seal on the deal
with some sort of, er... you know: poultry accomodation.
SILVERTONGUE
Wha... What's that? Who's this Sovereigntina?
PROMETHEUS
Sovereigntina? Why, she's the most beautiful thing,
a daughter of Zeus, she manages his store of thunder
and fulmination... and almost everything else, really:

good-counsel, good-order, sound-judgement, vituperation,
the ship-yards, the treasury, the public dole...

SILVERTONGUE

She's got the lot, then.

PROMETHEUS

Why, you're right: she's got it all... And if you get her from him,
you'll have it all – that's why I came here, to point-this-out,
for you know: I have always been a friend to men...

SILVERTONGUE

And how! Why, without you,
we'd have never even thought of the barbeque!

PROMETHEUS

...and I'm rather cold on the gods, you know.

SILVERTONGUE

Yes, by Zeus, you've turned your back on them completely.

PROMETHEUS

Just so. But now it's time for me to go... Here, give me the parasol,
I'm expecting a shower any time now.

SILVERTONGUE

A bridal shower? – Better yet, here: take this potty too,
and even if Zeus does see you... he might just think
you're a bee-keeper, just carrying a honey-pot – for Pooh!

PROMETHEUS

Oh, that's good. A Pooh-bearer, you mean?

SILVERTONGUE

Precisely!

PROMETHEUS

Not a stool pigeon?

SILVERTONGUE

Absolutely not! No wings!

PROMETHEUS (TAKES THE POTTY)

No wings! Farewell, Christopher Robin!

SILVERTONGUE
Godspeed, Pooh!
(EXEUNT)

CHORUS
In the desert land of Topsy Turvy
where they use their feet as a parasŏl,
there is a swamp where many a god-denier
tries to conjure up a living soul!
Sokrates went there once, unclean and scurvy,
to seek his guiding spirit in the moat,
and as sacrifice, like Ulysses once did it,
he cut a baby camels throat!
He took a step back, then up from below,
– lured by the camel's blood there in the mire –
came his buddy Chairephon,
one part leech, the rest: vampire!

ENTER POSEIDON, HERAKLES, AND TRUMPIANUS

POSEIDON
This is it, Colleagues, this metropolis, as far as the eye can see,
is Cloudcuckooland, the object of our embassÿ... (TO TRUMPIANUS:)
What're you doing, Trumpy? Draping your cloak over your left arm?
Can't you put it on your right, so they can plainly see...
we're not here to cause them any harm?
TRUMPIANUS
Cum to bear 'em arm!
POSEIDON
No, bare 'em arm! – If we "bare 'em arm"
they'll think we're bearing arms, good god, you savage, what next?

TRUMPIANUS TRIES TO ADJUST HIS CLOAK, BUT MERELY EXPOSES HIS OVERSIZED PHULLUS

O Democracy, where wilt thou lead us in the end,

if the gods can elect a prick like this –
understudied and oversexed!
(ADJUSTING THE TRUMPIAN'S CLOAK) Hold still! Oh, god damn!
You are the most barbaric god I have ever seen!
Come now, Herakles, what should be our plan?

HERAKLES (WRINGING HIS CLUB, AS IF TO CHOKE IT)
I'm thirsty... for pay-back! Let's put-the-squeeze on him,
this maniac... who walled us off from the flow of sizzling juices.

POSEIDON
But, my good fellow, we have been chosen to mend the fences
with this man... not to wring him out.

HERAKLES
Fences? All the better to hang him on, I say.
But first we wring him dry, then let's see what that produces!

SILVERTONGUE ENTERS, ACCOMPANIED BY SLAVES WITH A BRAZIER, A TABLE, AND COOKING UTENSILS. HE SETS ABOUT MIXING A FEW THINGS IN A BOWL

SILVERTONGUE
You there, stir up those coals! Hey, someone fetch the cheese!
And where's the cheese-grater got to? And where's the silphium?

POSEIDON
The gods bid thee greetings, good gentle, er... bird – the three of us!

SILVERTONGUE
But I'm in the middle of a dressing, if you please.

HERAKLES
Hmm, that meat: what's it frum?

SILVERTONGUE
Some birds who rose up against the common-market
– the bird-market – they thought wrong.

HERAKLES
So that's why you're, ah... dressing them before us?

SILVERTONGUE
Addressing? Yes, a bit of a dressing down, you might say.
(LOOKS UP FOR THE FIRST TIME) O greetings, Herakles, what's up?

POSEIDON
Er, hem, we have come as ambassadors about the war, us...
from the gods, about a reconciliation of differences,
and an end to hostilities.
SILVERTONGUE (SHAKING A FLASK NEAR HIS EAR)
That sounds like an empty vessel... We're out of sesame...
(TO A SLAVE) Go grab some more... oh, and fetch the pestle.
HERAKLES
Oh, that sucks! You can't cook, keep, or catch a bird
without a little seed!
SILVERTONGUE
Yes: it won't succeed, you might say.
POSEIDON
Indeed – ahem: And as we have no interest in being at war,
and if you were at peace with us, or good friends as we were before,
we would grant you guarantees... of rain water in the wetlands,
and of course, er... consequently, an eternal supply of worms.
Concerning all of these things we come as plenipotentiariës,
with full powers to come to terms.
SILVERTONGUE
Yes, well, in the first place, we never initiated war against you...
and we're now willing to make peace, if indeed you
are now willing to do... what's right. What's right however is this:
The sceptre now held by Zeus might, er... no: must be given back
to us, the birds... and if reconciled on this thing,
I invite the ambassadors to come dine with me.
HERAKLES
Well that smells, er... that all seems just fine with me.
POSEIDON
What? You devil! You're a blockhead and a glutton.
Are you out to undermine your father?
To rob him of the sceptre: the rod that rules?
SILVERTONGUE
Really? Won't you gods be mightily unburdened

if we birds are the ones who're burdened by
having to have our, er... "hands on-tools"?
Why, as it is now, hiding themselves beneath the clouds,
the mortals – stooping as if to pray – forswear you anyway.
But if, however, you... had us birds as allies,
then when anyone tried to get away with lies,
swearing "by goose or by Zeus, as now they do... the gander,
waddling past the false-swearer in silent approach,
could fly-up and gobble his goolies off – in on-the-spot reproach!

POSEIDON (RECOILING, AS IF HIT IN THE GROIN)
Ooh, by Poseidon, what a good point... well taken!

HERAKLES (HAVING RECOILED ALSO)
Ooh, I feel the same way!

SILVERTONGUE (TO TRUMPIANUS)
Well then, Trumpy, what do you have to say?

TRUMPIANUS
Yer, Zilfatuk, bai gulees!

SILVERTONGUE
You see? Even he agrees. And now, let's say some human makes a vow
to offer some god, er... a cow... but then, being a greedy sod,
does a Sokrates, saying, "with all the time in the world,
patient is the god" – you know: quoting the old proverb –
and so he holds back that fatted calf... breaks his vow... renegs –
well, we'll be on hand to go collect the debt – on your behalf!

POSEIDON
Oh, I'll bet! Now, pray tell how: it usually takes an earthquake
to get more than a couple of eggs – let alone a fatted cow!

SILVERTONGUE
Why, "pray tell", that's just what I mean! That's why the eagle,
hawk, falcon, kite, and owl... are known as birds of pray...
So here's the scene: the false-oath-taker is counting out
his ill-gotten gains, or better still: in the bath, let's say...
so while his pants are down, his goose is cooked,
for now a raptor swoops – and snatches it all away...

then up to the heavens he flies, and delivers it up to you!
HERAKLES (TWIRLING HIS CLUB)
What do we need a sceptre for anyway?
I vote we give it back to them.
POSEIDON
Well, okay... better ask the Trumpian too.
HERAKLES (POKING THE TRUMPIAN WITH HIS CLUB)
Hoi, Trumpy-anus, what do you think about copping it sweet?
TRUMPIANUS
Yo-no-swit-n-sticki-whacka.
HERAKLES (SMILING)
He says he likes the smell of that meat.
POSEIDON
Well, that's two votes, so it doesn't matter how I feel.
HERAKLES (TO SILVERTONGUE)
Okay, that puts a seal on the sceptre deal...
SILVERTONGUE
Yes, that part of the deal is done... but there are just a couple
of other things that spring to mind, if we're going to avert more strife...
for though I give Hera over to Zeus – that's Item One –
we can't consumate this deal unless the girl Sovereigntina...
is given up to me – that's Item Two – as wife.
POSEIDON
Gadzooks, it's not reconciliation you're looking to consumate,
you, er... (TO THE OTHERS:) *Let's go back home again.*
SILVERTONGUE
Godspeed, gentle... er... (SAMPLING THE SAUCE) *Cook,*
the sauce is a little too sweet.. Let's have more curry...
HERAKLES
O holy human, Poseidon, what's the hurry?
Are we going to fight a war over one single female?
POSEIDON
Better than going to war over one single married one.

HERAKLES
Well, it's not like it's never been done... but I say we take a piece,
er... let's make our peace. Come on: let's hand her over.
POSEIDON
What, you sod? Can't you see you're being played for a sucker?
You're actually arguing against your own best interests –
and those of every god... For if perchance Zeus should shuffle off
his immortal coil... you – having given sovereignty to the birds –
will be left with nought... and you'll have to get a job, and toil
to make ends meet. But as it is, you know, if Zeus pops his clogs,
you stand to inherit "the farm and fort", as they say.
HERAKLES
The farm and fort?
POSEIDON
The farm and fort. The lot. Everything he's got...
SILVERTONGUE
Oh my, what the... come with me. (LEADING HERAKLES ASIDE)
You're being led down the garden path, can't you see?
You're not what you always thought!
Here, let me set you straight. You see, legally...
you have no claim to farm, nor fort.
Your uncle – is leading you astray... for, by law, you're
not, er... you're not, er "legitimate issue", as they say.
HERAKLES
What? Not legit?
SILVERTONGUE
That's right: Not legit. A bastard.
HERAKLES
What? A bastard? – Me?
SILVERTONGUE
Yes you, indeed... being, by Zeus, of a mortal woman begot.
How else do you think Athena would get to be called "the Heiress"
– though Zeus's son she's not... if she had a legitimate brother
standing first-in-line?

HERAKLES
But can't a father bequeath it all to a bastard, you know,
as his dying wish... even if his mam's a concubine?
SILVERTONGUE
Nope! It's against the law! Why, Poseidon here –
who's now setting you up to fail – he's first in-line, my boy...
he'd hold-out against you in any claim you made,
he'd assert himself as a brother, of the same mother,
the Real McCoy... full-blood, as a spade is to a spade...
I'll even quote the law of Solon for you, which you can hear
every day (ad nauseam!) in any Athenian court:
Er, hem... "If there be children, a bastard shall not be heir...
but if there be no legitimate issue... the estate shall pass
to the next of kin."
HERAKLES
Well, that sounds fair... So what do I get, by Zeus?
SILVERTONGUE
You? You get nought...
HERAKLES
Nought?
SILVERTONGUE
Nought. Now tell me, has the old man inducted you in...
er, to The Fraternity yet?
HERAKLES
The Fraternity?
SILVERTONGUE
Yes, you know: the tribe, the elders, the Olympians...
HERAKLES
Oh yes: No, he hasn't, actually – and I've always wondered about that.
(HE LOOKS SKYWARD, FROWNING)
SILVERTONGUE
Well, don't fret – though that's a bit of a snub,
but all the same: come on over to our frat...
I'll set you up as cock-of-the-roost,

and we'll furnish you with the cream-of-our-crops
(RUBS THE UNDERSIDE OF HIS CHIN) – *literally!*
HERAKLES
Well, as before, to me you seem to be laying a just claim,
to which your recent words have given a boost,
and for mine – concerning the girl – I say we give her over to you.
SILVERTONGUE (TO POSEIDON)
What then say you?
POSEIDON
I say nay.
SILVERTONGUE
The whole matter rests with the Trumpian then.
Hey Trumpy, what do you say?
TRUMPIANUS
Hmm, givem preety gurlee an' bik soberinces for burts.
HERAKLES
He says to give her away.
POSEIDON
By Zeus, he certainly didn't say to give her away.
HERAKLES
But he's speaking pidgin.
POSEIDON
Precisely, so what he did say was clearly for the birds,
and on this matter, I swear, these are my final words!
SILVERTONGUE
Good, so we're agreed that it's clear,
and that he said he gives her over to the birds!
POSEIDON
Agreed? To give her over?
SILVERTONGUE
Yes: agreed. You agreed he's speaking pigeon...
and that his vote was "clearly for the birds"
Oh, and you swore that those were your final words!

HERAKLES
Yes, a sacred oath, by Democracy, and you swore it.
POSEIDON (EXASPERATED)
I said... oh, never mind: I did give my word, I can't ignore it.
So you two work out the details: I shall be silent.
HERAKLES
Well, silence is consent, so it seems we have a deal –
and you a new fi'ancee! – Just come with us yourself to Heaven,
so as to take a hold of Sovereigntina and... well,
whatever else takes your fancy!
SILVERTONGUE (INDICATING THE NOW THOROUGHLY SEASONED POULTRY)
Well – and by some serendipitous ornithomancy –
these meats are all dressed and ready to be cooked,
all set for a wedding meal!
HERAKLES
And while you're gone, if you please, I'll stay here to do the cooking!
POSEIDON
Yes, but I'd sooner trust a starving mouse
to safeguard that block of cheese – so you'd better come with us.
HERAKLES
Hmm, cheese: I wouldn't mind a slice...
POSEIDON
Yes, well, that's all very nice... but nevertheless,
beggars can't be choosers, so I suggest
you find yourself a paying job, and knuckle down...
SILVERTONGUE (CLAPS TWICE)
Okay, let's go! – Now, someone fetch me a wedding gown!
(EXEUNT)

1ST HALF-CHORUS
In the land of Reporting
2ND HALF-CHORUS
In the land of Extorting

FULL CHORUS
near the law-court clock,
there thrives an unscrupulous by-tongue-glutting race:
1ST HALF-CHORUS
Yes they reap, sow and vint...
2ND HALF-CHORUS
Yes they rob, twist and mint...
FULL CHORUS
with their tongues:
2ND HALF-CHORUS
They fluck pigs too!
1ST HALF-CHORUS
They pluck figs too...
FULL CHORUS
They're a race of barbarian,
1ST HALF-CHORUS
The Silvertongue and the Trumpian,
2ND HALF-CHORUS
rhetorician and politician,
FULL CHORUS
and thanks to these by-tongue-gluttors,
1ST HALF-CHORUS
both those of the Silver- and well-forked tongue,
2ND HALF-CHORUS
who make deserts like the Tribulati,
FULL CHORUS
everywhere in Attika
1ST HALF-CHORUS
the tongue, like a victim, is diced and sliced,
2ND HALF-CHORUS
men are loyal to power and party,
FULL CHORUS
and the truth is sacrificed.

◇◈◈◈ THE WEDDING ◈◈◈◇

HERALD
O ye achievers of complete success,
greater than words your happiness,
O ye thrice-blessed wingéd race of birds,
receive now your "sover-wren", for here he comes,
approaching his blesséd citadel, so radiant that no
star was ever seen to shine so golden-bright –
nor does the cloudbusting flare of the sun's rays shine through so.
Yes, here he comes, one-of-a-kind 'mong men and birds,
brandishing the wingéd missile of Zeus, the thunderbolt,
and at his side... a bride... her beauty surpassing words.
The uncanny scents of springtime pervade both high-and-low,
as wreaths of fragrant vapours waft along on aromatic plume,
and the most spectacular sights of nature put on their show
– like showmen – for the beautiful bride and handsome groom.
And here they are themselves! Part the way ye yeomen! –
and let the divine Muse add her sacred voice – in song of happy omen!

A DAZZLING SILVERTONGUE ENTERS, FIRING-OFF THUNDERBOLTS,
ACCOMPANIED BY SOVEREIGNTINA, STUNNING, & IN MAGNIFICENT REGALIA

CHORUS LEADER
Get back! Stand aside! Clear out! Make way!
Oh wha-ho! wha-ho! Wow wee!
She is more beautiful than words can say!
Well, now let's fly around the lucky swine, 'round he
of blesséd fortune: Come, form up a cavalcade!

THE CHORUS DANCES IN SWIRLING CIRCLES AROUND THE ROYAL COUPLE

Okay, done! Now attention!
Form up the reception committee!
Oh what a happy marriage thou hast made:
the perfect marriage for this city!
CHORUS
Great and mighty things are come to the race of birds

thanks to this here man in the midst of the arena,
but now with bridal songs, and by the hymen-hymn,
let's receive him now just like a king –
him and his Sovereigntina!

CHORUS LEADER

To Olympian Hera was he of the towering throne,
great and first of the gods – and father of Athena –
once joined-abed by the Fates in hymen-hymns like this.
So let us sing... O Hymen! O Hymenai-o!

CHORUS

O Hymen! O Hymenai-o!

CHORUS LEADER

It was flourishing Eros of love's golden arrow,
who held the reins – and they were astraining! –
who kept Zeus on the straight-and-narrow...
not riding shotgun, he steered the carriage
to the hearth of Hera, and onto the path – of marriage!

CHORUS

Hymen, O Hymenai-o!
Hymen, O Hymenai-o!

SILVERTONGUE

I am delighted by the hymns, delighted by the songs,
(though the words are a bit of a cause for wonder...)
So come now, here before me, and sing a song – of thunder!
Sing a song in praise of how it shakes the earth –
Yes, I know: it's frightening! – and of the fiery thunderbolt
of Zeus, and of course this terrible and flashy lightning!

(HE FIRES-OFF ANOTHER THUNDERBOLT)

CHORUS LEADER (VOICE QUAVERING A LITTLE)

O great golden light of sky-borne thunder,
O fissile missile of a misguided Zeus,
O ye whose groaning spray the trembling earth lies under
as under the sky-god his earthly bride...
Hail ye with whom this fellow the earth now rocks –

having got the best of Zeus (and of his bonds and stocks!) –
all hail the charm-working Sovereigntina,
all the powers of Zeus there at thy side!

CHORUS

Hymen, O Hymenai-o!

CHORUS LEADER

O all ye tribes of together-flockers,
give yourselves over, now, to the wedding fest,
bearing wings (not arms!) to the grounds of Zeus
– and to the marriage nest!

SILVERTONGUE (TO SOVEREIGNTINA)

Grab my wings, O blesséd-one,
and hold me tight,
and let us dance together,
for I am going to lift you up
– let us take flight –
carefree we shall be,
our burdens all light as a feather!

DANCING TOGETHER, THEY FLY OFF TO A HIGHER CLOUD, WHICH DISSIPATES AS THEY EXIT THROUGH IT, REVEALING THE GOLDEN GLOW OF THE SUN. A RAINBOW APPEARS BETWEEN THE HIGHER CLOUD AND THE STAGE.

CHORUS

Ye-ha! Uto-pi-a!
The silver lining!
The pot of gold!
Now let us sing...
Hal-le-lu-jah!
Thy kingdom's come!
Hurrah! Hurrah!

– END –

Bibliography & References

A Greek-English Lexicon. Henry G. Liddell, Robert Scott, Oxford 1891

Ancient Greece, Martin, Thomas R., Yale University Press, 2013

Aristophanes Birds, Jeffrey Henderson, Harvard University Press, Cambridge, Massachusetts 2000

Aristophanis Comoediae Tomvs I. F.W. Hall, W.M. Geldart (eds.), Oxford University Press, Oxford 1906

Aristophanis Fabvlae, Tomvs I, N.G. Wilson, Oxford 2007

Dictionary of Greek and Roman Antiquities, William Smith (Ed.), Little, Brown, and Co., Boston 1859

Dictionary of Greek and Roman Biography and Mythology, William Smith(Ed.), Little, Brown & Co., Boston 1867

Dictionary of Greek and Roman Geography, William Smith (Ed.), Walton and Maberly, London 1856

Glossary of Proper Names

Many of the entries below refer to substitutions of recognizable modern names for obscure ancient ones made so as to offer something with a greater chance of dramatic immediacy and comic impact to modern readers and audiences than a footnote or scholarly conjecture. These have largely been marked with a leading asterisk, but since not even all conventional translations are strictly literal, it is often difficult to know whether an entry should be so marked or not cf. the entries on Silvertongue and 'Ripideasy...

Aegean, the sea separating Attika (q.v.) from Anatolia. I have used poetic licence to render the term "Trans-Aegean" in place of the phrase "Lydian or Phrygian".

Aeschines Αἰσχίνης, a boastful rhetorician and son of a sausage-seller whose aspirational proclivities far outmatched his actual talents, and whose name I have replaced with that of Donald Trump (q.v), on the assumption that it will provide a more enduring and immediately recognizable allusion than the original.

Aeschylus Αἰσχύλος, the celebrated tragic poet.

Aesop Αἴσωπος, the celebrated fablemaker, whose tale of *the Eagle and the Dung-beetle* (Ἀετὸς καὶ Κάνθαρος) contains a wealth of themes relevant to the current play.

Aetna Αἴτνη, a city founded in Sicily by Hieron of Syracuse, and celebrated in a poem by Pindar which is adapted and parodied here by Aristophanes.

Agamemnon Ἀγαμέμνων, the legendary Greek king.

Alexander Ἀλέξανδρος, *see* Paris.

Alimentary, a pun on the name of Halimous Ἁλιμοῦς, a town on the coast of Attika (q.v.), possibly named after some form of seafood cf. ἄλιμος "of the sea", "banishing hunger".

Alkmene Ἀλκμήνη, a mortal woman, mother by Zeus (q.v.) of Herakles (q.v.).

Alope Ἀλόπη, a mortal woman, mother of a child by Poseidon (q.v.).

Alpheios Ἀλφειός, eponymous god of a river whose panting was supposed to echo his heavy breathing in lust for the nymph Arethusa.

Ammon Ἄμμων, originally an African diety, usually represented with a ram's head, whom the Greeks associated to Zeus (q.v.), and whose oracle in the Libyan oasis of Siwah was highly valued.

Amphion, a son of Zeus (q.v.), reputed to have built magnificent structures by lifting the stones into place with the playing of his lyre. See the entry on Doric, below.

Aphrodite Ἀφροδίτη, Olympian goddess of (sexual) love, hence also of female beauty, carnal desire, etc.

Apollo Ἀπόλλων, one of the Olympian gods, the patron of light, science, truth, and hence "straight shooting" (with the bow). The similarity of his name with the verb ἀπόλλυμι (to destroy or kill), and his association with science, hence medicine, hence disease, may have led to the idea that Apollo would shoot down anyone mendacious enough to take his name and then break their oath. His prowess with the bowstring may have led to his association with the lyre, and hence to all music. The Paean, a song of praise originally sung for Paian (Παιάν, the physician and healer of Homeric times) came to be sung especially for Apollo, probably due to his association with medicine, yet – possibly because of his association with the bow and destruction – it became a song equally of triumph in war as of thanks for recuperation.

Ares Ἄρης, the Olympian god of War.

Artemis Ἄρτεμις, a goddess of robust health, virginity, and the bow and arrow. She was worshipped especially by women, and often associated with features of local geography like mountains and lakes, hence her many epithets, such as Κολαινὶς (exact meaning unknown).

Assembly Ἐκκλησία, a regular gathering of all male citizens, whose vote determined virtually all matters brought before it.

Athena Ἀθήνη, Ἀθηνᾶ, daughter of Zeus (q.v.), and patron goddess of Athens (q.v.); the virgin protectress of the city and of warriors; goddess of justice, wisdom, and handicraft.

Athens Ἀθῆναι, the principal city of Attika (q.v.), and home to Aristophanes and his audience.

Attika Ἀττική, the region of which Athens was the principal city.

Boeotia Βοιωτία. Its natives were stereotyped by the Athenians as gluttonous and clownish.

Chairephon Χαιρεφῶν, a close friend and follower of Sokrates (q.v.) whose pale complexion saw him likened to a bat (a creature of the night).

Chairis Χαῖρις, a musician who was evidently notorious for playing at sacrifices, and whose name became part of a proverb about bad playing.

Chaos Χάος, the original, undifferentiated state of things as imagined by the early Greeks.

Chorus Leader Κορυφαῖος, a role that I have, for dramatic expediency, followed others in distinguishing from the Chorus itself.

Chorus Χορός, about two dozen singers and dancers from whose collective identity the play takes its name. Aristophanes introduces each member of the chorus individually, by species, but some of these are not readily identifiable to modern scholars, so I have taken some liberty in identifying them as the Flamingo, Persian, (Motley) Hoopoe, Fatbelly-bird, Pidgeon, Godwit, Duck, Crane, Tattletail, Owl, Hoarder, Hunter, Diver, Hawk, Cuckoo, Redfoot, Redcap, Stork, Swan, Goose, Callingbird, French Hen, Turtledove, and Partridge. The costumes were probably both spectacluar and ridiculous. *Vivat comoedia!*

* **Christopher Robin**, hero of the stories by A. A. Milne, whose name and relationship to Pooh Bear (q.v.) I have used in the hopes of recreating the wonderful complex of witty invention in the exchange following line 1550 where, in the original Greek, our hero makes similar comedy at the expense of Prometheus' effeminate garb, but involving a different (though similarly scatological) pun on the props anciently carried in festive processions by young women and girls.

* **Christopher Wren**, the famous architect, whose name I have used as a meaningful and enduring substitute in the Herald's catalogue of well-known personalities with bird-like names following line 1292.

City on the Hill *see* Aetna.

Cloudcuckooland, a rendering of Νεφελοκοκκυγία that appears to have been first coined by John Wood Warter, in his translation circa 1830.

Corinthian Κορῐνθῐος, a native of Corinth, a city whose institutionalized (religious) prostitution lent the word, also, the meaning "courtesan".

Council Βουλή, a group of five-hundred citizens who managed the day-to-day business of the Assembly (q.v.).

Crete, substituted for Λέπρεος (q.v) into the rhyming version of the play so as to preserve Aristophanes' pun on the name of a locality familiar to his audience.

Cupid, *see* Eros.

* **Dan Quayle**, a former Vice-President of the United States whose name I have used as a meaningful, and hopefully enduring substitute in the Herald's catalogue of well-known personalities with bird-like names following line 1292.

Darius Δαρεῖος, one of the Great Kings of Persia (q.v.).

Delos Δῆλος, one of the Cyclades (islands of the Aegean, q.v.), birth-place of Artemis (q.v.) and Apollo (q.v.).

Delphi Δελφοί, site of a temple which housed a priestess of Apollo (q.v.), whose oracles were highly valued thoughout the ancient period.

Demeter Δημήτηρ, one of the great gods, sister to Zeus (q,v,) and Poseidon (q.v.) *et al*, she might best be thought of by us as Mother Nature herself…

Desire Πόθος, a personification represented elsewhere, along with Eros Ἔρως (q.v.) and Πειθώ Persuasion, as children of Aphrodite (q.v.).

Diagoras Διαγόρας, a philosopher and poet whose views on religion, and perhaps his birth on Melos (an island that had been beseiged and starved into submission by the Athenians) led him to flee Athens (q.v.), where a reward was subsequently offered for his return, dead or alive.

Dieitrephes Διειτρέφης, a contemporary of Aristophanes whose rise from a maker of wicker-bottles to the command of cavalry is inferred from lines 798 and 1440.

Dionysos Διόνυσος, often rendered merely as the god of wine, and often known as Bacchus, he is better understood as the god of the life-force, and hence of naturism, orgiastics, libido, inspiration, dance, drama, and comedy. He was both the god who inspired the festival of which this play was part, and the one in whose honour it was played.

Dodona Δωδώνη, site of possibly the most ancient oracle in Greece, where Zeus (q.v.) himself was believed to give messages to men through the rustling leaves of a sacred oak.

* **Donald Trump**, an outspoken self-promoter whose public record and career as a rabble-rousing politician have made his name synonymous with demagoguery and false claims. I have substituted his name for those of Aeschines (q.v) and Proxenides (q.v), among others, on the assumption that it will stand as an eduring semiotic for the sort of political and cultural cankers targetted throughout the play by our poet.

Doric, (in the context of this adaptation), one of the three great orders of classical architecture. I have used this to replace the original reference to Amphion (q.v.), so as to retain something of the allusion to the construction of temples for audiences unfamiliar with the background mythology.

Drachma Δραχμή, a unit of weight and coin.

* **Elon** (Musk), a man of fabulously inflated wealth whose name I have substituted for that of Theogenes (q.v), on the assumption that it will provide a more enduring and immediately recognizable allusion than the original.

Erebos Ἔρεβος, darkness, including that of the netherworld between Earth and Hades.

Eros Ἔρως, Love; entirely absent in Homer (q.v.), but in Hesiod and other early sources one of the primal forces of the universe, as also here according to our poet. The Cupid-like personification of this god is evidently a late development.

Euripides Εὐριπίδης, the celebrated tragic playwright. A favourite target of Aristophanes, who seems to have disliked his rationalizing style and use of pathetic subjects.

Exekestides Εξηκεστίδης, a contemporary of Aristophanes whose Athenian citizenship seems to have been brought into question (cf. line 764, where he is called "Karian" q.v.). I have repalced his name (and implied "backstory") with Jonah, the Wandering Jew (q.v.).

Fates Μοῖραι, one of the divinities thought to determine ones lot in life, destiny, etc.

Father Time, substituted for Kronos so as to take advantage of the modern "personification" with whose name (and provenance) he is often popularly conflated (cf. Κρόνος "Kronos" and χρόνος "time").

* **Florence Nightingale**, the famous "nurse" whose name I have used as a meaningful, and hopefully enduring substitute in the Herald's catalogue of well-known personalities with bird-like names following line 1292.

Fraternity φράτρα, a brotherhood or political association among the Greeks which, in the case of Zeus (q.v.) inducting Herakles (q.v.), would have indicated that the former had recognized the latter as his legitimate son.

Gaia Γαια *see* Mother Earth.

* **Gog** and **Magog** biblical names of the enemies of God's people who wage war against Him at the end of the world, but also, by historical conflation, of the giants who threatened the founding of the city of London. These names being widely used as metaphors for outsiders whose immense power represents an apocalyptic or existential threat to the body politic, I have substituted them for those of Kebriones and Porphyrion, two of the giants who fought the gods at Phlegra (q.v.). Magog also replaces Aristophanes' reference to "tyrants" at line 1075, where it is a metaphor for "boogey man", the tyrants being former kinglike rulers of Athens whose return was often mooted as a threat to the Athenian democracy.

Goodhope *see* Greenhorn.

Gorgias Γοργίας, a noted sophist and teacher of rhetoric.

Graces Χάριτες, goddesses of natural beauty, charm, creativity, goodwill, fertility, and happiness: Εὐφροσύνη (Joy), Θάλεια (Blossom), and Αγλαία (Beauty). They were initially consorts of Dionysos (q.v.).

Great King, any of the rulers of the Persian (q.v.) empire during the ancient period.

Greenhorn, my rendering of Ἐυελπίδης, as being a more natural sounding name, and perhaps an even better encapsulation of the general character of the part, than the literal "Goodhope". Unfortunately, only the commonly used transliteration "Euelpides" comes close to echoing the name of the famous tragedian (Euripides, q.v.), hence my interpolation of the name 'Ripideasy into the rhyming version of the Introductions, in an attempt to preserve the joke for an audience.

Hebron Ἕβρος, the largest river in Thrace (q.v.), and consequently in the consciousness and legends of the Greeks. (Orpheus was torn to pieces by the Thracian women on its banks.) Often mentioned in connection with the worship of Dionysos (q.v.).

Helen Ἑλένη, the most beautiful woman of ancient times, and wife of Menelaos (q.v.); her abduction by Paris (q.v.) precipitated the Trojan war.

Hellas Ἑλλάς, Greece.

Hera Ἥρα, the wife of Zeus (q.v.), goddess of marriage and motherhood, she is the very archetype of the wife and mother.

Herakles Ἡρακλῆς Ἡρακλέης, the divine hero of Greek (and later, as Hercules, of Roman) myth. His voracious appetite was often the target of comic caricature.

Hermes Ἑρμῆς, one of the Olympians; god of boundaries and crossings, guides, trespass, travellers, merchants, and luck; often represented with winged hat and sandals.

Hesiod, the famous poet, whose name I have interpolated into this adaptation to explain the uncredited allusion made by Aristophanes in the original.

Hestia Ἑστία, goddess of the hearth, fire, and hence of all sacrifices too.

Homer Ὅμηρος, the great poet of antiquity, believed to have composed the great epics of the Greek nation, the *Iliad* and the *Odyssey*, and a multitude of other poetry, all of which carried the weight of near-infallible authority. Sometimes referred to as *the* poet.

Hoopoe Ἔποψ, a bird with a long bill, large crest, and striped wings.

Hymen Ὑμήν, the god of marriages.

Iris Ἶρις, goddess of the rainbow; sometimes represented in ancient sources as the rainbow itself, sometimes as the messenger (go-between) of the gods, with the rainbow merely being the mark of her passage across the sky. The disrespect shown her by our main protagonist may stem from the fact that she is always represented as having a wide-flared tunic, and is even credited in late sources as having been the mother of the erotic Eros (q.v.) – possible hints that there are details in her myth of which we are not fully aware.

Itys Ἴτυς, son of Tereus and Prokne, killed by her in revenge for his rape and mutilation of her sister. Both Aeschylus (q.v.) and Sophokles (q.v.) mention him as an object of avian lamentation, with the song of some birds perhaps proverbially linked to his mourning.

* **Jeeves** *see* Manes.

* **Jonah**, my substitution for Exekestides (q.v.), with both the name itself, and the epithet I have taken licence to append (the Wandering Jew) giving something of the flavour of the allusions (and attitudes) to an outsider made in the original.

Kinesias Κινησίας, a well-known dithyrambic poet, notorious for his experimental style, personal appearance, and perhaps also his habits. He was the butt of criticism from many comic writers, and appears on-stage also in Aristophanes' *Lysistrata.*

Kleisthenes Κλεισθένης, a man often ridiculed by Aristophanes for effiminacy, and evidently a practitioner of depilation.

Kleokritos Κλεόκριτος, an Athenian leader of religious ceremonies, possibly famous for his lecherous ways, bird-like appearance, or effeminacy, whence the joke that he is a son of Kybele (q.v.), whose rites were orgiastic, and yet whose priests were apparently eunuchs.

Kleonymos Κλεώνυμος, a prominent Athenian whose posterity is almost entirely due to Aristophanes, by whom he was mocked in several places as a glutton, liar, and coward.

Korkurian Κορκυραῖα, of or from Korkura, evidently famous for the manufacture of double-thonged whips. Hence "Korkurian wings".

Krekopida Κρεκοπίδα, a neologism combining Κεκροπίδος "Kekropian" (an Athenian, a descendant of the mythical king Kekrops Κέκροψ) and κρέξ "kreks", a long-legged bird, perhaps a corncrake, but metaphorically "a noisy braggart". The possibility that the text should be amended to Κερκοπίδα "Kerkopida" would render a pun on Κέρκωψ "Kerkops", a mythical race of monkey-men (cf. κερκοπίθηκος "kerkopithekos", a long-tailed ape, a knave. One might also note that King Kekrops was also always represented with a long tail, albeit that of a serpent, and that the Kekropians were one of the ten hero-eponymous "tribes" of Athens).

Kronos Κρόνος, a son of Uranus (Sky) and Ge (q.v. Earth), youngest of the Titans (q.v.), father (by Rhea q.v.) of Hestia (q.v.), Demeter (q.v.), Hera (q.v.), Hades, Poseidon (q.v.), and Zeus (q.v.). Kronos unmanned his father and ruled the world in his place until he was in turn overthrown by his own son, Zeus.

Kybele Κυβέλη the Mountain Mother, a goddess whose worship spread from Anatolia into Greece, where she was assimilated to Rhea, and later Demeter (q.v.) and Aphrodite (q.v.). The mother of several gods, including Zeus (q.v.) and Poseidon (q.v.), her mysteries were closely associated with those of Sabazius (q.v.), and she seems to have had some specific association, also, with birds, as evidenced by a few oblique references in the current play, and by the later, wholly mysterious naming of the South American ostrich (the Rhea). The word στρουθός, translated here as "tit", could also be rendered "ostrich" (στρουθός μεγάλα, "big bird", as at line 874) or "hen", or with reference to a human, "lech", hence the joke about her being the mother of Kleokritos (q.v.).

Lakonian Λάκων, *see* Sparta.

Lampon Λάμπων, a well-known soothsayer and interpreter of oracles.

* **Larry Bird**, an American sports icon whose name I have used as a meaningful, and hopefully enduring substitute in the Herald's catalogue of well-known personalities with bird-like names following line 1292.

Leotrophides Λεωτροφίδης, a poet who, like Kinesias (q.v.), was evidently a proponent of the "new dithyramb", a style that was lampooned by comic writers as light, pallid, soft and thin, with some of these adjectives doubling as descriptions of the poets themselves.

Leto Λητώ, a rather obscure divinity except for the fact that she was the mother, by Zeus (q.v.), of Apollo (q.v.) and Artemis (q.v.), and hence mostly referred to in this role. Zeus evidently turned her into a quail, in which form she arrived on the island of Delos (q.v.), which thereby got the byname Ortuga ('Ορτυγία cf. ὄρτυξ a quail).

Lybia Λιβύη, North Africa (excepting Egypt).

Lydian Λυδός, a native of one of the Anatolian kingdoms just to the east of the Ionic Greeks, often enslaved, stereotypically stupid.

Magog *see* Gog and Magog.

Manes Μάνης, a common name for a male slave in Attic comedy. I have rendered this as Jeeves in the rhyming version of the play, as the latter conjures to modern ears, like Manes to ancient ones, the immediate identification of the character's status and role.

* **McCoy**, a name that really only ever appears in the phrase "the real McCoy", meaning "genuine".

Meander, god of the winding river of the same name, substituted for the river god Alpheios (q.v.), given that the former is recognizable to most moderns, and synonymous with the sort of to-and-fro' I have substituted into this adaptation for the panting implied by the original, and anciently associated with the latter in his lust for the nymph Arethusa.

Medias Μειδίας, a noted "quail-tapper" (ὀρτυγοκόπος) in a game where bets would be placed on the likelihood of quail escaping from a ring after being struck on the head. The similarity of this to cockfighting seemed to me to suggest Steven Seagal (cf. Steven Seagull, below) as a not unreasonable modern-day stand-in: thus to preserve something of Aristophanes' joke.

Megaword Μεγάβαζος, a Persian (q.v.) commander under Darius (q.v.), whose name is more literally translated as "Bigtalker".

Melanthios Μελάνθιος a tragic poet, attacked elsewhere by Aristophanes and others for gluttony, profligacy, and his offensive appearance. He may well have merely been dark-skinned (cf. μελανθής swarthy).

Melos Μῆλος, an island in the Cyclades, proverbial for the famine inflicted on the population by a ruthless Athenian blockade.

Menelaos Μενέλαος, the legendary king, brother to Agamemnon (q.v.).

Meton Μέτων, a famous geometer, astronomer, and mathematician. The Einstein of his day, he had been recruited to survey the colony proposed for Sicily, but had managed to avoid recruitment into the notoriously failed expedition.

* **Moe**(-hawk), an allusion to Moe Howard, the "silvertongue" of the comedy team The Three Stooges, and one of the most recognizable comedians of early cinema due to his distinctive bowl cut black hair.

Moros and **Lesbos**, two Greek islands whose names I have substituted into this adaptation so as to recover some of the humor and word play that is usually sacrificed by literal translations (which the interested reader can easily recover by reference to lines 145-154 in the companion interlineal to this volume).

(Mother) Earth Γαια (Gaia), Γῆ (Ge), considered the most primeval divinity in the pantheon, sprung from Chaos (q.v.), and mother of the Sea, Sky, and a host of other (mostly chthonic) divinities, titans, and giants.

Mountain Mother *see* Kybele.

Muse Μοῦσα, one of the goddesses of song, music, poetry, dance, drama, or of inspiration for any of the fine arts.

Nikias Νικίας, an Athenian general, whose caution and use of engines brought him considerable success, though at the expense of prolonged engagement. He was instrumental in negotiating the peace with Sparta that bears his name.

Oceanus Ὠκεανός, god of the great "river" supposed to encircle the earth.

Odysseus Ὀδυσσεύς, the fabled hero whose story, in epic form (the Odyssey), has been hailed as a masterpiece and credited to Homer (q.v.) since ancient times.

Olympian, in ancient times, one of the twelve gods said to inhabnit Mount Olympus (q.v.), not one of the participants in the Olympian games, held quadrennially in the city of Olympia hundreds of miles to the southwest.

Olympus Ὄλυμπος, one of the highest mountains in Greece, and reputed the home of the gods.

Orestes Ὀρέστης, evidently a notorious garment thief (snowdropper), whose name Aristophanes uses for an ironic contrast with his namesake, the legendary son of Agamemnon (q.v.).

Ortuga Ὀρτυγία, a byname of Delos (q.v.).

Paean παιών, a song of praise originally sung for Paian (Παιάν, the physician and healer of Homeric times) that came to be sung especially for Apollo (q.v.). Any solemn song, chant, or dirge.

Palsuasive *see* Silvertongue.

Pan Πάν, god of Arcadia and the pastural idyll, son of Hermes (q.v.); represented with goat's feet, horns, and shaggy hair; he was a favourite of Dionysos (q.v.).

Pandora Πανδώρα (Giver of All), here a byname of Ge (*see* Mother Earth), and not the woman who opened the box from which all the blessings of the gods escaped the posterity of mankind.

Paris (a.k.a. Alexander), the Trojan prince whose abduction of Helen (q.v.) – as his prize for having ajudged Aphrodite (q.v.) the most beautiful of the goddessses in a beauty contest against Hera (q.v.) and Athena (q.v.) – precipitated the Trojan war, and the siege of Troy.

Patrokleides Πατροκλείδης, a name associated with at least two decrees proposed at Athens, but whose posterity is somewhat tarnished by the incontinence of at leasst one of its bearers.

Peisander Πείσανδρος ("Persuasive man"), an Athenian whose machinations may have been instrumental in bringing on the war with Sparta – in which he played a role as general – and who would eventually lead a faction that overthrew the Athenian democracy. The play's main protagonist Πισθέταιρος ("Persuasive friend") may have been so named as a deliberate nod in this direction (q.v. Silvertongue).

Peisias Πεισίας, a fellow evidently known as "the Partridge" (πέρδιξ cf. πέρδομαι "fart"), possibly a traitorous gatekeeper.

Pelasgian Πελασγικός, name of some of the most ancient inhabitants of Greece, metaphorically of anything thought to be anciently indigenous.

Persian Μῆδος, Mede, the principal foreign enemy of the Ancient Greeks.

Philokles Φιλοκλῆς, a tragic poet, nephew of Aeschylus (q.v.) – and apparently something of an imitator of Sophokles (q.v.), having also written plays on the theme of Tereus (q.v.) and Prokne (q.v.) – thus explaining the joke at line 281.

Philokrates Φιλοκράτης, a name borne by a successful commander in the seige of Melos, but on the evidence of this play, evidently a reference, rather, to a prominent Athenian birdseller...

Phlegra Φλέγρα, "the place that's burning", site of the battle in which the gods overthrew the rule of the giants (the sons of Gaia, *see* Mother Earth); identified with any of a few different localities in ancient times that exhibited volcanic activity (and probably the occasional find of fossilized bones from large prehistoric animals).

Phrygian Φρύξ (acc. Φρύγα), a native of one of the Anatolian kingdoms just to the east of the Ionic Greeks, often enslaved, stereotypically stupid.

Phrynichos Φρύνιχος, one of the forerunners in the creation of the tragic genre, and cited by Aristophanes in several plays as an exemplar in the creation of beautiful melodies. I have substituted Pindar (q.v.) for him in this adaptation, assuming that he (Pindar) may be a less obscure reference.

Pindar Πίνδαρος, the greatest lyric poet of ancient Greece, referred to simply as *the* Lyricist, in much the same way as Homer (q.v.) was called simply *the* Poet, and Aristophanes *the* Comedian. I have used his name, also, as a substitute for that of Phrynichos (q.v.).

* **Pooh Bear**, hero of the stories by A. A. Milne, whose name not only lends itself to an easy scatological pun, but whose immediate recognition by an audience in connexion with the carrying of a pot is vital to the recreation of the humour inevitably to be lost in a literal translation of the exchange at hand. See also the entry on Christopher Robin, above.

Poseidon Ποσειδῶν, brother of Zeus, god of the sea, and perhaps thus of anything that causes the earth to shake, such as (pounding) waves, horses (by their hooves), earthquakes, etc. His trident will have somewhat recalled a pitchfork.

Potter's Field Κεραμεικός, the quarter of Athens where ceramics were made, but also where military funerals were held.

Priam Πρίαμός, the king of Troy, a favourite subject of an untold number of tragedies.

Prodicus Πρόδικος, a famous sophist.

Prokne Πρόκνη, a once human Athenian princess, married to Tereus, now the Nightingale. Her transformation into a bird had been an act of grace worked by Dionysos (q.v.) to prevent further violence following her killing of her own son, Itys (q.v.) in revenge for Tereus' rape and mutilation of her sister Philomela.

Prometheus Προμηθεύς (Forethought), not technically a Titan (q.v.), nor a god, he knows that Zeus (q.v.) – in punishment for his gift of fire to mankind – is looking to bind him to a rock in Tartaros (q.v.), where an eagle will devour his liver each day (it growing back each night).

Proxenides Προξενίδης, mocked as a boaster also in *Wasps*.

Pythian Πυθιάς, belonging to the priestess of Apollo (q.v.) at Delphi (q.v.).

Rhea Ῥεία, a goddess whose name I have substituted in for the word Kybele (q.v.), as being much easier for the English-speaking world to deal with.

'Ripideasy *see* Greenhorn.

* **Robin Williams**, an American comedian whose name I have used as a meaningful, and hopefully enduring substitute in the Herald's catalogue of well-known personalities with bird-like names following line 1292.

* **Russell Crowe**, a famous actor whose name I have used as a meaningful, and hopefully enduring substitute in the Herald's catalogue of well-known personalities with bird-like names following line 1292.

Sabazius Σαβάζιος, originally an Anatolian god, son of Kybele (q.v.), whose orgiastic rites saw him assimilated to Dionysos (q.v.).

Semele Σεμέλη, a mortal woman, mother by Zeus (q.v.) of Dionysos (q.v.).

Silvertongue, my rendering of Πισθέταιρος "Persuasive Friend"; a dramatic improvement over the more literal "Palsuasive", and a nice coupling with the rendering of Ἐυελπίδης as Greenhorn (q.v.). Though only the commonly used transliteration of the variant Πεισέταιρος "Peisetairos" captures the allusion to Peisander (q.v.) conveyed in the original, the reference to our main character's tongue accords well with the theme of the Tereus (q.v.) myth, and with Aristophanes' reinforcement of it by the stophe-antistrophe "couplet" of the Chorus at lines 1553-1564 and 1694-1705.

Sokrates Σωκράτης, the celebrated philosopher. I have, in this adaptation, used references to Sokrates as a substitute for the originals to Prodicus (q.v.) and Kleokritos (q.v.), as the essence of each reference is the jibing of a well-known personality, for which Sokrates, to most moderns, is almost the only contempory of Aristophanes who fits the bill. That Sokrates may not have been a sophist nor infidel did not prevent Aristophanes from using him as a semiotic for such things in this play and elsewhere.

Solon Σόλων, the celebrated statesman and legislator, whose reforms to the Athenian constitution were credited with laying the groundwork for the democracy and empire of the golden age.

Sophokles Σοφοκλῆς, the celebrated tragic poet, whose play *Tereus* (now lost) may have informed most of the audience about the Tereus-Prokne backstory alluded to in this play.

Sovereigntina Βασίλεια, the Greek means both "Princess" and "Sovereignty".

Sparatos, my licence for Spintharos (q.v.).

Sparta Σπάρτη, the capital of Lakonia, and the main city of the Peloponnese.

Spintharos Σπίνθαρος, a playwright accused by Aristophanes of being a Phrygian (q.v.), and by others of trying to pass one of his own plays off as the work of Sophokles (q.v.).

* **Steven Seagull**, a play on the name of Steven Seagal, an American actor whose name I have used as a meaningful, and hopefully enduring substitute in the Herald's catalogue of well-known personalities with bird-like names following line 1292. In particular, I have used him as a replacement for Medias (q.v.) because Seagal's martial-arts shtick has allowed me to make something of Aristophanes' joke about the quail-tapper (for which, see the entry on Medias, above).

Syracuse, an ancient and prosperous Greek (colonial) city in Sicily.

Tartaros Τάρταρος, according to Homer (q.v.), a place as far below Hades as Heaven is above Earth, and only in later times becoming synonymous with the lower world in general, and Hades in particular.

Teleas Τελέας, ridiculed elsewhere for incon-stancy, gluttony, and other vices. Aristophanes uses the root meaning of his name (τελέ- "bring to an end") in puns more than once.

Tereus Τηρεύς, a once human (non-Athenian) King, now the Hoopoe. His transformation into a bird had been an act of grace worked by Dionysos (q.v.) to prevent further violence following his crimes against his wife, Prokne (q.v.) and her sister Philomela, whom he had raped, then muted by the removal of her tongue. The Tereus myth was familiar to contemporary audiences through the works of Sophokles (q.v.) and others.

Thales Θαλῆς, a philosopher, revered (like Einstein) as the proverbial genius, but from a bygone time (he had forecast a solar eclipse, etc.).

The Apollonian τἀπόλλωνος, the (oracle) of Apollo (q.v.).

Theogenes Θεογενής, a public figure whose precise relationship to Aristophanes' jokes is now obscure, but who we can infer may have enjoyed at least the appearance of wealth, or success, with the racing of horses or chariots.

Thesmophoria Θεσμοφόρια ("the law-giving"), the festival of Demeter (q.v.), kept at Athens (q.v.) exclusively by the female citizenry. I have translated this elsewhere as "The Rites of Women".

Thrace Θρᾴκη, the part of Europe to the immediate north of Greece, and the scene of considerable military activity throughout the period.

Titan Τιτάν, any of the sons and daughters of Uranus (q.v.) and Ge (Gaia q.v.), including Oceanus (q.v.) and Kronos (q.v.).

Tranquility Ἡσυχία, a sort of divine personification, rather than an actual diety.

Triballi Τριβαλλοί, a barbarian tribe on the borders of Thrace (q.v.), also a cognomen facetiously applied to groups of troublesome young men who idled about taverns, hence my attempts to preserve the various connotations of the name with words like "tribal", "tribulation", and "Intemperates". See also the entry on Trumpianus.

Tribulati, my licence for the Greek Τριβαλλοί, q.v. Triballi.

Trumpianus, my licence for Τριβαλλός (Triballian, q.v. Triballi), a barbarian god invented by Aristophanes, I suspect, for the sole purpose of the bad grammar required to achieve ambiguity at lines 1681-82.

* **Turkey**, until recent times the English name for the nation now estrablished by the Turks over all of Anatolia (Asia Minor). The name change was evidently prompted by the Turks' realization of the other connotations of the name, which, though an anachronism, quite neatly replaces Aristophanes' complex pun on the rather obscure alternative name for (one of the ten tribes of) Athenians (q.v.), namely Kekropian Κεκρόπιος, the "descendants" of Kekrops Κέκροψ, a mythical king of Athens. See also the entry on Krekopida.

Ulysses, the latinized form of the name Odysseus (q.v.), which I have used in Part One in consideration of its familiarity to the ears of an English-speaking audience.

Uranus Οὐρανός, (personification of) the sky.

Victory Νίκη, a goddess usually conceived by the Athenians as an angel-like handmaid to Athena (q.v.) and Zeus (q.v.).

* **Walter Pidgeon**, an American actor whose name I have used as a meaningful, and hopefully enduring substitute in the Herald's catalogue of well-known personalities with bird-like names following line 1292.

Wisdom Σοφία, a sort of divine personification, rather than an actual diety.

Zeus Ζεύς, King of the Olympian gods, and father of many of them (and of several demigods, heroes, etc.) by various wives, mortal and divine. As ruler of heaven and earth, he is the dispenser of justice, fair weather (and foul), thunderbolts, etc.

Acknowledgements & Disclaimer

As previously, I have made considerable use of the many excellent digital resources available to students and researchers in the creation of this book, in particular the Perseus Digital Library of Tufts University, and have assiduously turned to the print works listed in the bibliography where doubts over particular points of meaning or relevance have arisen. Once again, I am very grateful to Alison Mutton for the cover illustration and artwork, despite the outrageous content one is compelled to include in an effort to do justice to the original author, and to the students and audiences for whom this book is intended.

www.ingramcontent.com/pod-product-compliance
Lightning Source LLC
Chambersburg PA
CBHW070502170726
48291CB00008B/2612

* 9 7 8 1 7 6 4 0 5 8 2 0 9 *